Handbook on Restructuring and Substantial School Improvement

Herbert J. Walberg, Editor

CENTER ON
INNOVATION &
IMPROVEMENT
Twin paths to better schools.

Center on Innovation & Improvement
http://www.centerii.org

INFORMATION AGE PUBLISHING
Charlotte, NC • www.infoagepub.com

Acknowledgement

The editor and leadership of the Center on Innovation & Improvement are appreciative of the suggestions made by representatives of the U.S. Department of Education's Regional Comprehensive Centers, U.S. Department of Education personnel, scholars, and educational leaders who have critiqued this Handbook at various stages, from concept to outline to draft. We are also grateful to the contributors to this volume and those who copy edited the manuscript and designed the publication, Pamela Sheley and Lori Thomas.

Center on Innovation & Improvement
121 N. Kickapoo Street
Lincoln, IL 62656 USA
Phone: 217-732-6462
Fax: 217-732-3696

www.centerii.org

Information • Tools • Training

Positive results for students will come from changes in the knowledge, skill, and behavior of their teachers and parents. State policies and programs must provide the opportunity, support, incentive, and expectation for adults close to the lives of children to make wise decisions.

The Center on Innovation & Improvement helps Regional Comprehensive Centers in their work with states to provide districts, schools, and families with the opportunity, information, and skills to make wise decisions on behalf of students.

A national content center supported by the U. S. Department of Education's Office of Elementary and Secondary Education.

Award #S283B050057

Contents

Library of Congress Cataloging-in-Publication Data

Handbook on restructuring and substantial school improvement / Herbert J. Walberg, editor.
    p. cm.
 Includes bibliographical references.
 ISBN-13: 978-1-59311-763-4 (pbk.)
 ISBN-13: 978-1-59311-764-1 (hardcover)
 1. School improvement programs–United States–Handbooks, manuals, etc.
I. Walberg, Herbert J., 1937-
 LB2822.82.H358 2007
 371.1–dc22

                                           2007020373

Printed in the United States of America

Preface

Herbert J. Walberg, Editor

As suggested by the title, the purpose of this *Handbook on Restructuring and Substantial School Improvement* is to provide principles for restructuring and substantially improving schools. Sponsored by the U.S. Department of Education, the Center on Innovation & Improvement (CII) engaged leading experts on restructuring and school improvement to prepare modules for this handbook to assist states, districts, and schools in establishing policies, procedures, and support to successfully restructure schools. The Handbook is organized into three sections.

Section 1: Overview of Restructuring

The Handbook complements *School Restructuring Under NCLB: What Works When?* produced by Public Impact and the Center for Comprehensive School Reform and Improvement (CCSRI). Written by three of the authors of that document, Bryan Hassel, Emily Hassel, and Lauren Morando Rhim, the introductory Overview of Restructuring explains the complementarities between their previous work and the present handbook as well as the meaning of the term restructuring. within the context of the federal No Child Left Behind Act (NCLB) and early research on the experience with restructuring thus far

District and school leaders must possess a steely will and a compass set firmly on children's learning to eliminate low-performing schools from a district, the Overview authors assert. The cross-industry and education literature makes clear that all efforts to effect dramatic change have the potential to create firestorms among stakeholders – from community members to parents to traditional interest groups – without regard to the potential benefit to children.

Section 2: Topical Modules

The six modules in the second section address NCLB and restructuring. Each module or chapter is useful in its own right but also helpful in combination with one another. Individuals may study and discuss the set of modules as a whole or combinations of modules depending on the circumstances, challenges, and opportunities they face. Because of their importance and because the modules are designed to function together as well as separately, some principles are discussed in more than one module.

As a guide to the content of the modules, the following paragraphs give the title, author, and essence of the six modules:

1. "District-Wide Framework for Improvement" by Kenneth K. Wong: To address accountability in the era of No Child Left Behind, district-led reform initiatives have broadened to governance and management reform, data-driven decision making, alignment of incentives and sanctions, and consumer-oriented services.
2. "The School Board and Central Office in District Improvement" by Gordon Cawelti and Nancy Protheroe: Both the pace and extent of improvements in student achievement can be substantially impacted by a systemic and coherent district-wide initiative focused on instruction and supported by strong district leadership.
3. "Restructuring Options and Change Processes" by Carole L. Perlman: In selecting a restructuring option, employ data, evidence-based practices, and knowledge of the change process.
4. "Restructuring Through Learning-Focused Leadership" by Joseph Murphy: Leadership requires developing a mission and goals, managing the educational production function, promoting an academic learning climate, and developing a supportive work environment.
5. "Changing and Monitoring Instruction" by Herbert J. Walberg: To improve achievement, focus instruction and assessment on state standards, employ assessment to evaluate students' progress, and employ instruction selectively to bring all students to proficiency.
6. "Systems for Improved Teaching and Learning" by Sam Redding: To implement and sustain substantially improved teaching and learning in the restructured school, systems must be in place to enable the people attached to the school to competently fulfill their roles and achieve clear goals, especially improved student learning.

Section 3: Indicators of Successful Restructuring

The third section of the Handbook provides checklists of specific actions for developing and implementing a successful restructuring plan. This section references the modules in the second section, and brings them together in a practical summary of best practices for restructuring and substantial school improvement. Parts of the section form an instrument that can be used for classroom observation and teacher interviews to assess instructional progress in restructuring schools. Evidence collected with the indicators can be used to identify needs and strengths of the restructuring process and the likelihood of substantial NCLB-required Adequate Yearly Progress.

Research Basis

Ideally and in accord with the U.S. Department of Education Institute of Education Sciences, education policy and practice should be based on well-conceived, well-executed randomized field trials (RCTs) at the district, school, classroom, and individual levels; these are "the gold standard" evidence. Short of experiments, well-done quasi-experiments and large-scale longitudinal studies, preferably following the progress of individual students, are desirable.

Much of educational research falls short of these standards, and the modules are based to a large extent on "promising practices," which blend findings from rigorous research in other fields, research and field expertise, statistically controlled, correlational studies, and long and outstanding records of improved performance.

The topic of the Handook's modules – restructuring with a focus on the district as the impetus for dramatic improvement – is relatively new in the nation's education history. For this reason, the module authors were selected because they are highly experienced experts in their fields and can be counted on to judiciously weigh the less than definitive evidence and to state useful guiding principles.

Introduction: Overview of Restructuring

Bryan C. Hassel, Emily Ayscue Hassel, and
Lauren Morando Rhim

Research on organizational restructuring and turnarounds from other industries provides useful information that should guide school restructuring efforts mandated under NCLB.

Abstract

Cross-industry literature on organizational restructuring that entails radical
change provides lessons that should inform school restructuring plans. This
chapter presents the lessons within the context of NCLB restructuring mandates and identifies specific links between the seven modules and that research
as summarized in *School Restructuring Under No Child Left Behind: What Works
When? A Guide for Education Leaders,* published by the Center for Comprehensive School Reform and Improvement.

No Child Left Behind Restructuring

Under the federal No Child Left Behind Act (NCLB), schools that do not
make Adequate Yearly Progress (AYP) for five consecutive years are required
to develop plans for "restructuring" in the sixth year. If they fall short of their
state's academic targets again, they must implement those plans the following
year. NCLB offers five options for schools in restructuring:

1. reopen the school as a public charter school;
2. replace "all or most of the school staff (which may include the principal)
   who are relevant to the failure to make adequate yearly progress";

---

3. contract with an outside "entity, such as a private management company, with a demonstrated record of effectiveness, to operate the public school";
4. turn the "operation of the school over to the State educational agency, if permitted under State law and agreed to by the State"; or
5. engage in another form of major restructuring that makes fundamental reforms, "such as significant changes in the school's staffing and governance, to improve student academic achievement in the school and that has substantial promise of enabling the school to make adequate yearly progress."(No Child Left Behind, Sec. 1116, 20, U.S.C.A. §6301-6578; 2002)

Non-regulatory guidance from the U.S. Department of Education in 2006 further defines this fifth "other" option to include reforms such as:

- changing the governance structure of the school either to diminish school-based management and decision making or to increase control, monitoring, and oversight by the LEA;
- closing the school and reopening it as a focus or theme school with new staff or staff skilled in the focus area;
- reconstituting the school into smaller autonomous learning communities;
- dissolving the school and assigning students to other schools in the district;
- pairing the school in restructuring with a higher performing school; or
- expanding or narrowing the grades served.

Who is Restructuring Under NCLB?

Though NCLB's restructuring provisions are certainly not the nation's first foray into seeking dramatic improvement in chronically low-performing schools, the federal law has sparked restructuring activity on an unprecedented scale. During the 2005-06 school year, approximately 600 schools nationally were implementing restructuring plans under NCLB (Center for Education Policy [CEP], 2006a). Most states have not been tracking AYP long enough for schools to enter restructuring. These numbers, however, are likely to grow dramatically. According to the CEP, only about 15 percent of schools in improvement in 2004-05 exited improvement status in 2005-06 (2006a). With the other 85 percent continuing to head toward restructuring, nearly 2,000 schools may well be in restructuring in 2007-08, rising to 3,200 in 2008-09.[1]

In 2005-06, most schools in restructuring (90%) were in urban districts; nearly half were in just 15 such locations (CEP, 2006a). Schools in restructuring tend to serve traditionally disadvantaged populations. In 2004-05, for example, 60 percent of students in restructuring schools qualified for free or reduced-price lunch – compared to 41 percent of all public school students, 40 percent were Hispanic, and 37 percent were African-American – compared to 19 and 16 percent, respectively, across all public schools (Le Floch, Taylor, & Zhang, 2006). In line with the number of elementary versus middle and high schools, most schools identified for restructuring to date are elementary schools. However, when considered as a proportion of total number of schools, a greater number of middle schools have been identified for restructuring than either elementary or high schools (Le Floch et al., 2006; National Center of Education Statistics, 2005).

Which Restructuring Options are Districts Using Now?

Recent surveys suggest that most districts are primarily implementing "option 5" restructuring (LeFloch et al., 2005). In Michigan, for example, 93 percent of restructuring schools in 2004-05 used option 5 (CEP, 2005b). In 2005-06, 76 percent of restructuring schools in California pursued option 5 (CEP, 2006b). The Center on Education Policy found that in districts using these moderate interventions, 42 percent appointed an outside expert to advise the restructuring school; 24 percent extended the school day or year; 14 percent "restructured the internal organization of the school" (CEP, 2006a). Almost no districts invited private firms or state agencies to take over restructuring schools or reopened schools as charter schools. Of schools implementing more drastic reforms, the most common approach was to replace staff members, who would have been difficult to replace without the power of federal sanctions, with other staff considered more qualified to teach in these schools. Fourteen percent of all restructuring schools replaced some or all staff members in 2004-05 (CEP, 2006a; Dibiase, 2005).

Research on Restructuring: What Works When?

At the request of the Center for Comprehensive School Reform and Improvement (CSSRI), Public Impact reviewed the existing research on restructuring across industries and organizational types. This review defined "restructuring" as changing the very structure of a chronically failing organization in an attempt to spur dramatic improvement (Hassel et al., 2006). While rigorous research on this phenomenon in K-12 education is fairly limited, there is a more extensive research base examining restructuring in other kinds of public sector agencies, nonprofits, and private companies. The review resulted in a series of four white papers on each of the first four NCLB restructuring options as well as a guide for district leaders on choosing among the restructuring options and launching the restructuring process (Arkin & Kowal, 2006; Kowal & Hassel, 2006; Kowal & Arkin, 2006; Steiner, 2006).

Three broad lessons emerged from this review, as well as a series of more specific findings (CCSRI, 2006a). **First, *large, fast improvements are achieved by different methods from incremental changes over time.*** Strategies that work to create big change are quite a bit different from strategies typically used to improve organizations that are already working pretty well. Most notably, successful, large improvements are preceded by a change in the *direction and control* – and how direction and control are used. In schools, this means getting the right leader in each school and the right kind of oversight by the district or external providers chosen by the district. The right leader can effect enormous improvements no matter how low the odds of success. However, *replicating and sustaining* large improvements appears unlikely without major governance changes by a whole district.

In the cross-organizational experience, when performance moves from very low to adequate or high, it is typically through one of two mechanisms: turn-arounds or fresh starts. In a turnaround, the organization's leader (usually a new leader) takes action to transform organizational performance substantially and rapidly. Though the leader may replace some staff, the hallmark of a turnaround is that it is largely the same organization achieving dramatically better results. In a fresh start, by contrast, a new organization is formed in place of the old one. By doing things differently from the start rather than asking existing staff to make changes, the new organization achieves substantially better outcomes than the unit it is replacing.

It is easy to see how fresh starts are different from standard "school improvement" efforts, which focus on enhancing the performance of existing school organizations. Successful turnarounds are also quite different from incremental change. Specifically, successful turnarounds tend to be managed by *leaders with particular capabilities* who pursue a *well-defined set of turnaround actions* – points to which we return in a moment.

Second, *eradicating chronically low performance is not a one-time project; it is a commitment that is a core part of school and district work.* Even the most effective, dramatic restructuring strategies, the ones that work when nothing else has, fail sometimes. Thus, the same organizations must sometimes undergo repeated restructuring to achieve desired success. Roughly 70% of turnaround efforts – those aimed at turning bad organizations to great from within – fail across industries (Kotter, 1995). In the private sector where success and failure is relatively simple to measure, investors expect roughly 20% of start-up organizations fail and another 60% bump along with mediocre performance; only 20% are very successful (Christensen, & Raynor, 2003). Yet as noted above, these two strategies – turnarounds and fresh starts – are the only two that cross-organization research has shown to work for *replacing very low performance* with *very high performance.*

Cross-industry surveys of top managers indicate that regular, major restructuring is an expectation in highly competitive, achievement-oriented industries (Kanter, 1991). Districts that want to replace low-performing schools with significantly higher performing ones will need to adopt the same expectation. Major restructuring will be a regular event, not a one-time activity, for districts that both serve large numbers of disadvantaged children and succeed in having *no chronically bad schools.*

With each round of restructuring, some schools will improve dramatically, others will improve a great deal but not quite enough, and others will continue to fail. Many districts have become facile at helping relatively strong schools make continued, incremental improvements over time – a good strategy for schools that improve a great deal after restructuring. But what about schools that continue to fail? District leaders must set clear performance goals and commit to identifying and promptly addressing continued failure: additional restructuring attempts in these schools will be essential (e.g., introducing a new turnaround leader, changing charter or contract providers, or choosing another restructuring option entirely). Creating a pipeline of promising turnaround leaders and contract/charter providers may be a necessary companion activity for long-term elimination of very low-performing schools.

Third, *district and school leaders must possess a steely will and a compass set firmly on children's learning* to eliminate low-performing schools from a district. The cross-industry and education literature makes clear that all efforts to effect dramatic change have the potential to create firestorms among stakeholders – from community members to parents to traditional interest groups – without regard to the potential benefit to children. It is all too easy for leaders to seek to avoid these controversies by shying away from significant restructuring. In successful organizational improvement, by contrast, leaders find ways to include stakeholders in the process without letting them divert it from success. That process takes a strong unbending will and a compass set determinedly on children's learning.

Beyond these broad lessons, the review of cross-organizational literature revealed specific findings that can inform efforts at school restructuring. In particular, successful efforts to dramatically improve struggling organizations tend to follow these principles:

- **Provide governance** of the restructuring process. Good governance ensures that the rest of the ingredients are included in the mix. In the school context, this means a strong and appropriate role for the district and state in the renewal effort.
- **Manage stakeholders.** Stakeholders can break a change effort without regard to the potential benefit for children in a school, and they can enable change when they support it. Managing stakeholders well is a key differentiator of successful efforts to improve organizations.
- **Create the right environment for leaders of restructuring organizations.** The most critical environmental factors include:
  - **Freedom to act** very differently from past organizational practice and from other organizational units. Organizations that achieve dramatic improvements shun enormous temptations to let efficiency, consistency, prior relationships, staff, customer and community preferences, and political concerns trump what's best for organizational results. They make big changes that work, even when inconvenient or uncomfortable.
  - **Accountability** that is clear, frequently tracked, and publicly reported. If measurement systems are inadequate, improving them rather than failing to monitor is the solution for success.
  - **Timeframes** that allow plenty of time for planning changes but very *short* timetables to demonstrate success on a limited number of targeted goals. *Successful*, big changes all get results fast. Results should be clear after one year. Speedy support of successful strategies and quick elimination of failed strategies happens only when timeframes are short. Longer term work is required to extend success and make it sustainable, but the initial burst of achievement is a hallmark of successful efforts at dramatic improvement.
  - **Support that helps without hijacking** organizations' freedom to do things very differently. In the school context, financial, human resource, technical, data, and other service support from the district is critical, as is coordination among these functions when needed to allow deviations by a school in restructuring. But help should be provided with great care not to compromise changes that school leaders need to make (e.g., in how money is spent, school schedule, curriculum, teaching approach, student progress monitoring, and the like).
- **Choose the right leaders and manage them the right way.** According to cross-organizational research, leaders who are effective in restructuring are different from leaders who are successful maintaining and improving already high-performing organizations. Successful start-up leaders resemble entrepreneurs, and successful turnaround leaders combine the characteristics of

entrepreneurs and traditional organization leaders. They also take actions that may differ from the actions leaders take in incremental change situations. For example, effective turnaround leaders focus relentlessly on a small number of high-priority goals in order to obtain quick victories that, in effect, teach the organization how to win. While culture change precedes results in incremental change efforts, culture change tends to follow these early wins in turnarounds. Importantly, these leaders do not do everything themselves: they motivate staff and other stakeholders (e.g., students and parents in the school context) to higher levels of performance. They utilize the talents of staff, external consultants, and others to balance their own strengths and get the job done.

- **Ensure organizational practices:**
  - **Effective school practices:** Schools where students learn more than similar students in other schools employ effective practices very consistently, and this has been well-documented in repeated research.
  - **Staffing:** Teachers and other staff who support change and implement effective school practices are essential. Whether drawn from existing staff or hired from outside the preexisting school, staff members willing to do what works to ensure that children learn are critical.

Together, these cross-organization research findings provide helpful broad guidance to school, district, and state leaders interested in successful restructuring. Since they are broad-ranging, however, they do not provide the kind of detailed guidance leaders also need in order to plan for and implement restructuring. The modules in this Handbook take that critical next step. The following section previews those modules, noting how they align with the cross-industry literature on successful restructuring and substantial improvement.

Connecting Links: Handbook Modules and the Research on Restructuring

In Module 1, Kenneth Wong discusses the importance of district-wide improvement to supporting the effective implementation of school level best practices. This module complements the lessons culled from cross-industry literature regarding the central importance of governance changes by a whole district to implement, replicate, and sustain the right restructuring environment. The module stresses the importance of establishing partnerships with quality intermediaries and engaging key constituencies (e.g., civic and community leaders, parents, and teachers) to support district restructuring efforts. Intermediaries can introduce unique skills and expertise to the district. Civic and community leaders introduce "civic capacity" that district leaders can use to garner support for initiatives that are painful for stakeholders but necessary for the overall strength of the community.

The principle related to exploring a diverse provider model is an example of a relatively radical change in direction and control that reflects the lessons that emerged from the cross-industry literature. In the diverse provider model, districts willing to "grant management autonomy" hire contractors to provide services through performance contracts with measurable outcomes. Contractors may provide specific programs or manage entire schools. Introducing external providers to the education process represents a significant alteration to the manner in which a district functions, in that the central office shifts from operating schools to monitoring and holding external providers accountable. While not without risk, this model holds the potential of leveraging outside capacity to promote innovation and raise performance in low-performing schools without increasing costs. Based on the cross-industry literature, successfully introducing external providers will require the district to select providers carefully, provide appropriate support, grant enough organizational freedom for the new operators to make the required changes to implement their models, and hold operators accountable for results.

In Module 2, Gordon Cawelti and Nancy Protheroe focus on the role of the school board and central office in district improvement. The module's principles closely parallel the cross-industry research on how system-level governance and the broader environment can influence the success of organizational restructuring. One of the key parallels is the module's emphasis on the importance of the resolve of top leadership in pressing for change and improvement, characterized as "relentlessness," "intensity," and even "missionary zeal." Another is the focus on setting ambitious targets for improvement, both short-term and ongoing, followed by continuous use of data to track progress over time. The module also echoes the literature in stressing resource reallocation: searching for efficiencies and making tough tradeoffs rather than simply adding on new funds. Finally, the module points out the importance of engaging parents and the wider community, who the research suggests can make or break efforts at serious change.

One of the module's principles focuses specifically on intervening in low-performing schools, and that principle's key ideas closely follow cross-industry research on governance of restructuring. The module lays out a set of district practices most likely to help failing schools turn the corner, including: "having the right people in place" via staff reassignment or turnaround principals, providing tailored support, offering selective flexibility (such as waivers from district policies to allow a principal to move teachers), and establishing incentives and sanctions for performance on a clear timeline. All of these approaches find solid support in the literature on creating a strong environment for organizational turnaround.

In Module 3, Carole Perlman examines the various restructuring options articulated in NCLB, charts the change process, and recommends key resources for practitioners. This module moves beyond identifying effective practices and articulates the steps necessary to plan for and engage in successful restructuring. The module acknowledges that multiple paths can be taken to radically change a school but, echoing the research culled from the cross-industry literature, notes that developing an intentional and strategic approach is critical to success. The strategy should reflect the unique district context, and the specific programmatic and curricular models should be based on rigorous research. Furthermore, also embracing cross-industry findings, the module stresses the importance of governance, planning, and committing to continuous improvement after a school's performance becomes satisfactory.

The module's first five principles emphasize the importance of not only preparing for radical change but understanding schools' strengths and weaknesses in order to select a restructuring approach and, thereafter, develop a feasible plan. Reflecting the cross-industry literature related to maintaining a compass set on student learning, the module stresses the importance of allocating resources "to support the school's instructional priorities." Principles six through eight move beyond the broad definition of restructuring to discuss more specific NCLB options: charter school conversions, contracting, and turnarounds via new leaders and staff. These principles provide helpful guidance about unique features of each of these restructuring options and provide links to tools that practitioners can access to learn more about the options and build upon preexisting knowledge bases.

While NCLB allows multiple means of restructuring, the cross-industry literature emphasizes the critical importance of choosing the right leaders to implement restructuring plans regardless of the option chosen. In Module 4, Joseph Murphy reviews decades of research related to school leadership in general. The module identifies key attributes of "learning-focused leaders" who successfully concentrate on instruction in order to ensure that other dimensions of schooling support "robust core technology and improved student learning." Specifically, the module defines the components of learning-focused leadership as leadership committed to developing mission and goals, managing the education production function, promoting an academic learning climate, and developing a supportive work environment. Though the research evidence suggests that leadership in restructuring carries some different demands from general school leadership, numerous themes in the module's review match the cross-organizational literature about leading substantial improvement.

The principles related to developing mission and goals – especially with regard to articulating, translating, and stewarding the vision – parallel the research base related to the imperative school leaders' unyielding focus on student learning. Murphy describes learning-focused leaders as working "ceaselessly to promote the schools' mission and agenda." Furthermore, in accord with the literature related to promptly addressing failed efforts, learning-focused leaders are "careful monitors" who don't shy away from identifying shortcomings and failures. Learning-focused leaders also forge a positive climate by setting high expectations, becoming personally engaged in change, and providing incentives for staff and students to excel – all hallmarks of successful leadership in restructuring.

In Module 5, Herb Walberg draws from a broad and deep research base to describe instruction and assessment principles that should serve as the heart of school restructuring plans. The module is guided by three core principles: means must be aligned with end goals; resources must be allocated to monitor and focus practice toward the goal of proficiency for all students; and parents are critical partners to success so schools should strive to support and improve the "curriculum of the home." In sum, echoing the cross-industry literature, this model demonstrates that in order to effectively restructure, classroom instruction must be guided by specific goals that are constantly monitored, and if necessary adjusted, and supported by targeted allocation of resources that create the right environment for success.

The principles related to formative and summative assessments mirror the cross-industry literature related to committing to a fast cycle of continual improvement. Rather than relying on a single annual test to assess practice, the four principles related to testing admonish schools not only to align instructional with state standards, but also to integrate standardized tests and frequent classroom assessments as key sources of data to inform and shape classroom practice. By regularly assessing student progress, teachers can quickly identify areas for improvement and re-teach topics and skills. In line with the cross-industry literature regarding mid-course corrections, assessments enable teachers to reallocate time and resources while remaining focused on the goals of proficiency for all students. Regardless of whether a school opts to restructure by converting to charter status, hiring an external contractor, or recruiting a leader skilled at turnarounds, the principles related to instruction and monitoring should be a central component of the school restructuring plan.

In Module 6, Sam Redding describes the process of continuous improvement in the restructuring school. This module complements and extends Module 5 by describing how restructured schools can integrate changing and monitoring instruction in a systemic manner that supports not just classroom but school-wide improvement. For entire schools to be successful, they must embrace the notion of regular and continual monitoring of progress supported by teams (e.g., leadership, instruction, and school community) that are empowered to act. The module emphasizes the importance of engaging teachers in goal setting, aligning standards and assessments, and monitoring improvement in order to ensure that teachers embrace collective responsibility for school improvement and have the skills required to support success.

The principle related to the school leader's role in the building and capacity echoes the cross-industry literature related to the critical importance of selecting the right leaders and managing them the right way. The principle describes the effective restructuring leader as an individual who is a "change agent more than a manager" and a "fire carrier for the school's vision." The effective leader sets tangible and attainable goals that enable the school to document early successes, which are characterized as "seeds of large-scale success." These seeds of success mirror the early wins that the cross-organization literature says are vital to teach failing organizations "how to win," fostering long-term improvement.

In the final module, Sam Redding integrates the information presented in the preceding six modules and outlines "Principles and Checklists of Success Indicators" that districts can use to plan, implement, monitor, and sustain school restructuring. Reiterating the importance of district and school collaboration and focus, parental and community engagement, and disciplined, competent implementation, the module provides 12 detailed checklists related to issues such as: establishing district conditions for school improvement, using data to develop an evidence-based improvement model, articulating specific roles and responsibilities of district and school personnel, engaging teachers, and thereafter monitoring their performance. Echoing the lessons culled from the cross-organization literature, these checklists demonstrate the importance of hiring the right leaders with unique capabilities; managing them the right way so that they can focus on key priorities; and thereafter committing to establishing and maintaining the environment required to ensure quick, substantial change that, once established, can be sustained for long-term success.

Endnotes

[1]Analysis based on current trends reported in Center on Education Policy, *From the Capital to the Classroom.*

References

Arkin, M. D., & Kowal, J. K. (2006b). *Reopening as a charter school.* Washington, DC: Center for Comprehensive School Reform and Improvement.

Beer, M., & Nohria, N. (2000, May-June). Cracking the code of change. *Harvard Business Review,* 133-141.

Center on Education Policy. (2006a). *From the capital to the classroom: Year four of the No Child Left Behind Act.* Washington, DC: Author. Retrieved November 20, 2006 from http://www.cep-dc.org/nclb/Year4/CEP-NCLB-Report-4.pdf.

Center on Education Policy. (2006b). *Wrestling the devil in the details: An early look at restructuring in California.* Washington, DC: Author.

Center on Education Policy. (2005a). *From the capital to the classroom: Year three of the No Child Left Behind Act.* Washington, DC: Author.

Center on Education Policy. (2005b). *Hope but no miracle cures: Michigan's early restructuring lessons.* Washington, DC: Author.

Christensen, C. M., & Raynor, M. E. (2003). *The innovator's solution: Creating and sustaining successful growth.* Cambridge, MA: Harvard Business School Press.

DiBiase, R. W. (2005). *State involvement in school restructuring under No Child Left Behind in the 2004-05 school year.* Denver, CO: Education Commission of the States.

Hassel, E. A., Hassel, B. C., Arkin, M. D., Kowal, J. K., & Steiner, L. M. (2006). *School restructuring under No Child Left Behind: What works when? A guide for education leaders.* Washington, DC: Center for Comprehensive School Reform and Improvement.

Kowal, J. K., & Hassel, E. A. (2006). *Turnarounds with new leaders and staff.* Washington, DC: Center for Comprehensive School Reform and Improvement.

Kowal, J. K., & Arkin, M. D. (2006). *Contracting with external education management providers.* Washington, DC: Center for Comprehensive School Reform and Improvement.

Kanter, R. M. (1991, May-June). Transcending business boundaries: 12,000 world managers view change. *Harvard Business Review,* 151-164.

Kotter, J. P. (1995, March-April). Leading change: Why transformation efforts fail. *Harvard Business Review, 73*(2), 19-27.

Le Floch, K. C., Taylor, J., & Zhang, Y. (2006). *Schools in NCLB restructuring: National trends.* Washington, DC: American Institutes for Research.

National Center for Education Statistics. (2005). *Participation in education.* Washington, DC: Author.

No Child Left Behind Act, Sec. 1116, 20, U.S.C.A. § 6301-6578. (2002) (enacted).

Steiner, L. M. (2006). *State takeovers of individual schools.* Washington, DC: Center for Comprehensive School Reform and Improvement.

U.S. Department of Education. (2006). *LEA and school improvement: Non-regulatory guidance.* Washington, DC: Author.

About the Authors

Bryan C. Hassel is Co-Director of Public Impact, a national education policy and management consulting firm based in Chapel Hill, NC, and a member of the Center on Innovation & Improvement's Scientific Council. Dr. Hassel has conducted extensive research on restructuring chronically low-performing schools and other organizations. He is co-author of School Restructuring Under NCLB: What Works When? A Guide for Education Leaders, as well as numerous other publications on revitalizing low-performing schools. Dr. Hassel is engaged in several restructuring projects for the Center on Innovation and Improvement, including advising the U.S. Department of Education on a study of school turnarounds and providing technical assistance to states on NCLB restructuring. He also consults nationally on a range of education reform issues, including school finance, teaching quality, and charter schools. He received his doctorate in Public Policy from Harvard University and his master's in Politics from Oxford University, which he attended as a Rhodes Scholar.

Emily Ayscue Hassel is Co-Director of Public Impact. Ms. Hassel previously worked as a consultant and manager for the Hay Group, an international human resources consulting firm. At Hay, she worked with a variety of industries in the public and private sectors, where she helped clients manage people more effectively to achieve desired organization results. She is currently leading several national projects designed to build the capacity of states and districts to respond to chronically low-performing schools and to build teacher and leader capabilities. Her other work in education includes: authoring the North Central Regional Education Laboratory's *Professional Development: Learning from the Best*, a toolkit on designing and implementing high-quality professional development based on the experiences of model professional development award winners; co-authoring *Picky Parent Guide: Choose Your Child's School with Confidence*; creating NCREL's comprehensive website on professional development; and authoring people-management training tools for a public school leadership institute organized by SERVE, the Southeastern regional educational lab. Ms. Hassel received her law degree and Master in Business Administration from the University of North Carolina at Chapel Hill.

Lauren Morando Rhim is a Senior Consultant for Public Impact and a Technical Advisor for the Center on Innovation & Improvement. Dr. Rhim previously held a research appointment at the University of Maryland, College Park in the College of Education where she directed a national research study on charter schools and, specifically, issues pertaining to students with disabilities in charter schools. She also worked closely with the National Association of State Directors of Special Education on multiple research and technical assistance projects designed to assist state, district, and school policy leaders to develop capacity to deliver special education and related services in charter schools. In her other education work, she recently completed a comprehensive evaluation of charter schools in Maryland for the Maryland State Department of Education. She consults with multiple national organizations on school reform issues and most recently completed a series of case studies examining state-initiated school takeovers for the Education Commission of the States. Dr. Rhim received her doctorate in Education Policy from the University of Maryland, College Park and her master's in education from The George Washington University.

1. District-Wide Framework for Improvement

To address accountability in the era of No Child Left Behind, district-wide improvement initiatives have broadened to governance and management reform, data-driven decision making, alignment of incentives and sanctions, and consumer-oriented services that contain the elements of restructuring for individual schools when that becomes necessary.

Abstract

The No Child Left Behind Act of 2001, with its high stakes accountability, poses challenges and opportunities to school systems. Do districts have the capacity to meet standards-based accountability? How can district-led initiatives facilitate data-driven decision making? To what extent are districts able to align their incentives and sanctions to support accountability? What are some of the promising district strategies to raise student performance? In short, how can districts maintain a system-wide infrastructure of support for schools and teachers in the current climate of accountability? This module considers these questions by examining the literature on system-wide initiatives and efforts to promote school improvement.

Introduction

The No Child Left Behind Act of 2001 (NCLB) created a framework on educational accountability for all children. In many ways, NCLB represents an unprecedented level of system-wide direction in core elements of public education, and it promises federally mandated restructuring if schools fail to reach the performance goals. The federal law requires annual testing of students at selected elementary and high school grades in core subject areas, mandates the hiring of "highly qualified teachers" in classrooms, and grants state and local agencies substantial authority in taking "corrective actions" to turn around failing schools. Further, the law provides school choice to parents to take their children out of failing schools and supplemental educational services (tutoring) for students in failing schools. Equally significant is the legislative intent in closing the achievement gaps among racial/ethnic subgroups as well as income subgroups. All in all, NCLB places districts in a pivotal role in both district-wide improvement and in the improvement, correction, and restructuring of individual schools.

Principles

1. Build technical capacity at the district level with periodic, standards-based assessments

The No Child Left Behind Act has generated the need for data-driven decision making in school districts. Traditionally, school districts maintain an evaluation and research unit primarily for regulatory compliance. Annual reports on student progress are mandated by federal and state agencies for financial auditing and for meeting civil rights provisions. Categorically funded programs, such as special education and Title I, have their subsystems of assessment criteria, test administration, and reporting. Fragmentation in data organization has contributed to problems of inaccessibility, coordination, and accountability. In large urban districts, even the superintendents encounter difficulties in gaining full access to the district's entire data base that connects students to their classroom teachers.

Black and Wiliam (1998) argue in an extensive literature review that teachers should use formative assessments to better understand the needs and difficulties of their students to adapt the curriculum to serve their students' needs best. The authors report that there is substantial evidence to assert that initiatives focusing and strengthening the use of formative assessments often observe substantial learning gains. They also report that in situations with many low-performing students, the use of formative assessments can raise underperforming students' achievement and also improves achievement for the entire group, with effect sizes between 0.4 and 0.7 in the experiments they observed. The authors state that through the use of feedback, teachers can modify their teaching and learning standards for all of their students.

The Achievement Council in Los Angeles, California, uses disaggregated data to have meetings with parents and students to guide policy. The parents and students have a central role to play in school change, which can contribute to improved community life. The students, parents, and teachers have monthly meetings to go over assessment data to drive changes in equity within the schools. The organization is able to provide support to better understand data, explore equity issues, provide professional development for teachers and administrators, and help build parent and student capacity. Through this, they hope to foster increased engagement for everyone involved with the school, including parents and students.

In Horry County, South Carolina, administrators and teachers began using student achievement data in the early 1990s, which led to their discovery of a difference in test scores for students that had enrolled in their preschool program. Seventy-five percent of students who enrolled in the preschool program were scoring higher on the third grade assessment. After their discovery, the district expanded the program to allow for more students to enroll, which led to higher group scores in the third grade.

In light of the necessity for disaggregating student achievement by subgroups to meet NCLB expectations, school districts are turning to external organizations to help build the data analytic infrastructure. An example of a periodic assessment system that can be employed district-wide is the Northwest Evaluation Association, whose computerized assessments with "vertical scales" can be administered to students up to four times a year. The NWEA data base of 6,000 schools across the country enables districts to locate the appropriate comparison group for gauging student progress. With multiple measures within the school year, teachers, schools, and the district can track progress leading to the state assessment and make instructional corrections along the way to address each student's assessed learning strengths and deficits.

2. Enlist district-intermediary partnerships

District reformers have looked for intermediaries, organizations that work between the district and the school and in collaboration with both, to build district and school capacity; Marsh, Kerr, Ikemoto and Darilek (2006) examine how district-intermediary partnerships promote system-wide instructional improvement. In their study of the Institute for Learning's (IFL) work in three urban school districts, the authors found that implementation of research-based strategies faced numerous challenges as the IFL tried to scale up its efforts. Particularly, the school districts struggled with flexibility and ownership over initiatives. Yet, demonstrating the reach of the reforms, they also found evidence of new ideas and concepts moving into the everyday language of district administrators and school-level personnel, including teachers. The district-level, third-party intermediary helped infuse these concepts and ideas into the district, providing a common basis for communicating about and determining the effectiveness of improvement strategies.

Chicago has broadened the scope of intermediary partnerships. Chicago's Renaissance 2010 plan consists of the creation of charter schools, contract schools, and new CPS performance schools. All three types of schools are publicly funded by the Chicago Public Schools. However, the three types of schools operate with significantly different degrees of autonomy. Only the charter and contract schools can be said to be operated by diverse service providers, since performance schools are small schools that operate under similar restrictions as CPS schools and are fully administered by CPS. The charter and contract schools, on the other hand, are administered by their own autonomous school boards or by outside educational management organizations. CPS charter schools have autonomy in curriculum design, teacher and principal hiring, and compensation. Their curricula must meet state standards, and they must be specified in the charter plan. CPS contract schools have autonomy in curriculum design, but they are required to hire only certified teachers. Contract school curricula must meet state and CPS standards and must be specified in the Performance Agreement signed with CPS. Importantly, the Chicago Public Schools-Chicago Teachers Union collective bargaining agreements explicitly do not apply to charter teachers, whereas they do apply to performance school teachers. Organizations involved in the program include community-based nonprofits, groups of long-time CPS teachers, national educational management organizations, and the Chicago Teachers Union.

3. Institute district-wide strategies to affect classroom instruction

Districts are devoting their professional development resources to support strategies that create professional communities at the school level. Wong and Nicotera (2006), for example, examined the implementation of a peer coaching initiative in several schools in a low-performing district. They found that peer coaching supported teachers as they aligned state standards and assessments to classroom practices. They found that participating teachers reported greater integration of state standards into their instructional practices and greater attention to standards-based assessments in guiding their instructional planning than a set of control schools not using peer coaching. Their analysis reveals that while elementary and middle schools were able to use coaches to support teachers' work, the high school faced the most obstacles to meeting set goals. This study demonstrates the challenge of implementing district-level professional development initiatives across schools and the promise of district-initiated peer coaching strategies where properly applied.

4. Build civic support for school reform and restructuring

When a district develops a restructuring plan for a failing school, community involvement and support are essential. When the district operates within a framework of civic and community responsibility for school success, the difficult options of restructuring meet with greater support and understanding. Political scientist Clarence Stone (2003) introduced the notion of "civic capacity" as a strategy to mobilize broad-based formal and informal stakeholders' support to place public education on a city's institutional agenda. Civic capacity is needed to address the confidence gap within the school community. In a 1998 survey, for instance, the National School Boards Foundation found that "there is a consistent, significant difference in perception between urban school board members and the urban public on a number of key issues" (National School Boards Foundation, 1999, p. 12). While 67 percent of urban board members surveyed gave their schools As and Bs for their level of quality, only 49 percent of the urban public surveyed did. Moreover, whereas three out of four board members rated their teachers as excellent or good, only 54 percent of the public agreed. In recent years, mayoral involvement in urban education can be seen as an institutional effort to fill this public confidence gap (Wong, 2006). Mayors often see an improving public school system as a key social indicator for urban livability and a political signal to the private sector that the city is committed to a human capital strategy. Chicago's Mayor Richard Daley, for example, sees a good school system as an "anchor" for families and neighborhoods.

From the viewpoint of public engagement, mayors can galvanize widespread support since they hold a broader mandate than the city's elected school board. For example, a typical mayoral election receives a 45 percent to 55 percent voter turnout, which is several times more than a typical nonpartisan school board election. In New York City, just prior to the passage of the state legislation that granted Mayor Bloomberg control over the school district, fewer than 5 percent of eligible voters turned out to cast ballots in the local community school board elections. Similarly, in Chicago there was a continuous decline in turnout for the election of local school council (LSC) members: Between the first LSC election in 1989 and 1993, the last one before mayoral takeover of the district, there was a 68 percent drop in parent turnout. By contrast, when a mayor is granted the power to appoint the school board, he or she can focus on mobilizing electoral support for school reform. In Boston, after Mayor Menino named seven members to the first mayor-appointed school board in 1992, he subsequently proclaimed himself an "education mayor." Later on, 54 percent of the Boston electorate opposed a 1996 referendum that called for a shift back to an elected school board. That election saw an unusually high voter turnout of 68 percent.

5. Build community and parental support for school reform and restructuring

When school improvement is elevated to a matter of civic responsibility and pride, municipal officials, in concert with school officials, are able to communicate directly and effectively with broad swaths of the public and also to assist in reaching parents in particular schools, such as those in restructuring. Parental engagement is an area where mayors can make a difference. Under the No Child Left Behind Act, for example, districts are required to issue annual report cards on district and school performance in making Adequate Yearly Progress (AYP). When schools do fail, parents have the right to transfer their children to higher-performing schools. Under this system, schools and school districts face the challenge of making sure that parents – particularly in disenfranchised neighborhoods – receive the necessary information about their children's educational options in a timely manner. In these situations, mayors use their various communication channels to connect parents to schools more efficiently. In other efforts to enhance parental engagement, many cities work with employers to enable parents to take their children to classes on the first day of the new school year. Cities such as Nashville, Tennessee, have gained corporate commitments to donate supplies and backpacks the weekend before the start of the school year. City Hall and the nonprofit sector also have implemented strategies that encourage inner-city parents to attend parent-teacher conferences and pick up their children's report cards. By enlisting municipal offices in support of its improvement efforts, districts create a broad base of community support and understanding for dramatic measures such as restructuring when they become necessary.

6. Maintain communication and coordination throughout the system

The system within which a district operates is larger than the district itself and includes the municipal, state, and federal agencies that impact upon the district, as well as the array of community groups that it contains. As external pressure to raise school performance rises, there is an urgent need for the district leadership, schools, and key civic and policy stakeholders to communicate and coordinate on their decisions on governance, finance, curriculum, professional development, and management. In districts where schools enjoy discretion to select their own reform models, or in conditions of restructuring where the restructuring plan of the specific school breaks beyond the bounds of standard district policy, coordinating efforts across the district can pose a challenge. The district curriculum office, for example, needs to facilitate links and keep lines of communication open between the schools and the district, thereby maintaining the balance between support and pressure. The superintendent also needs to articulate his/her vision on school improvement to the larger community on an ongoing basis.

Communication turns more complex in the context of NCLB expectations as implementation involves multiple layers of government. Facing local and state reluctance, the U.S. Department of Education has relaxed certain requirements on a case by case basis. An example of intergovernmental accommodation is Chicago's success in gaining federal approval to provide tutoring programs for students in schools that failed to make AYP. Under NCLB, districts that do not meet AYP, including most large urban districts, are prohibited in providing supplemental instructional services after school to their students. The U.S. Department of Education required that Chicago replace its own services with outside vendors in January 2005. Mayor Daley stepped in and put his political capital behind the CEO's decision to continue the district services. In a series of private meetings between the Mayor and the U.S. Secretary of Education Margaret Spellings, compromise was reached. In return for the district's continuation of its supplemental services, the city agreed to reduce barriers for private vendors to provide tutorial services. When the compromise was formally announced by Secretary Spellings in early September in Chicago, Mayor Daley hailed the efforts as the "beginning of a new era of cooperation" across levels of government in education (see Dillon, 2005, p. A11). A similar waiver was subsequently granted in New York City. Clearly, intergovernmental negotiation can smooth the implementation of NCLB in complex urban systems.

A policy challenge is for the district leadership to serve a dual function, namely as a "critical friend" to schools in need of improvement and as a buffer to leverage external resources and pressures. An example is Trenton, New Jersey, one of the poorest and lowest performing districts in the state that is classified as an *Abbott* district (one of the 28 poorest districts in the state which received reallocation of funds in response to a 1994 decision of the New Jersey Supreme Court). Two central office positions, City and Community Liaison Services Coordinator and Director of Curriculum, keep communication between the city and central office continuously open and allow policy coordination between city hall and the district. In recent years, Mayor Douglas Palmer, who has the power to appoint the school board, had a hand in the buyout of two superintendents, as well as an active role in hiring James Lytle as superintendent. Palmer and Lytle met regularly to discuss Lytle's district-wide reform ideas and decisions (Wong, Buice, & Cole, 2006). The close linkages among the school board, district administration, and city hall made it possible for

Lytle to replace three under-performing principals. The mayor and the superintendent also worked together closely to testify and lobby on an emergent school facilities bill in New Jersey that would provide Trenton with $320 million for improving school facilities.

7. Develop civic-district strategies for improvement

Through extensive interaction among Trenton's senior administrative group and the Trenton Board of Education, school communities, employee organizations, and the New Jersey Department of Education (DOE), Trenton came up with a strategy to turn the district school system into a more effective institution. Among the key efforts were to:

- Take a creative approach to areas in which the New Jersey DOE was unsure about how to move ahead, such as school-based budgeting, preschool program implementation, and facilities planning.
- Keep elected officials – including the mayor, city council, and their legislative delegation – informed and unified with regard to local education issues.
- Emphasize the district mission of insuring that as many students as possible who enter ninth grade complete high school and go on to college, work, or military service. Lytle reminded all teachers, administrators, and others involved in the reform process that what the Trenton community and parents wanted – over and above achieving higher test scores – is for their children to develop into adults who are responsible and self-supporting.
- Reduce or eliminate the long-standing problems of the district – alarming drop-out rate, high incidence of special education referrals, high failure rates on state tests – as well as improve on the undue use of suspension as a discipline strategy, and deal with the high rates of retention and course/subject failure.
- Remove school principals and teachers who cannot lead reform, and replace them with ones who can – this entailed recruiting a cadre of young and minority administrators with strong moral purpose and strong backgrounds in instructional leadership.

8. Align coherent incentives

Arguably one of the most controversial reforms is to connect teacher performance to the level of compensation. While economist Milton Friedman proposed the notion of differential pay as a strategy to increase teacher responsiveness to parent "consumers" over 40 years ago, recent studies point to promising effects of bonus pay to recruit and retain qualified teachers in challenging schools. Research found that experienced teachers tended to migrate from schools with higher percentages of low achievement, low income, and minority populations. However, teacher transfers can be reduced in the presence of financial incentives even in schools with a higher concentration of at-risk students. This is particularly crucial when a restructuring plan seeks to replace ineffective staff with higher quality staff.

In recent years, several districts and states began to implement bonus compensation to attract qualified teachers to challenging instructional settings. For example, Hillsborough County, Florida, began a bonus program for "qualified" teachers who were willing to relocate to schools with lower performance. Qualified teachers are those who earned a master's degree, gained several years of experience, and received a National Board of Professional Teaching Standards certificate. In return for their move to the low-performing schools for one year, teachers earn an extra compensation that roughly amounts to 20 percent of their salary. The district is able to fund this initiative by reallocating its staff development budget. In Denver, a recent initiative (ProComp) that has received public support in a local funding referendum weighs differential staffing responsibilities and accomplishments in assigning extra compensation.

Further, districts provide extra compensation to qualified teachers who are willing to teach in areas of high demand, such as schools in restructuring. In Houston, teachers earn a $5,000 bonus for working in subject areas that are in need of qualified teachers. In Los Angeles and Houston, extra bonuses are used to attract teachers to teach ELL students. Utah provides $5,000 for math and science teachers who agree to teach in the public school system for four years. Consistent with these recent developments, districts and universities are forming new partnerships that allocate tuition fellowships to students in teacher training programs. In return, graduates of these university programs are required to teach in the public schools for a certain period of time. Examples of these district partnerships include institutions such as Yale, Duke, NYU, and CUNY, among others.

9. Explore a diverse service provider model

The diverse service provider model allows a district to outsource specific elements of school operation or contract for the operation of whole schools, with different providers engaged to fit the needs of the school. The diverse service provider model is attractive to urban districts for several reasons. Bushweller (2003) observed that the popularity of this model can be attributed to five factors: "a history of outsourcing for special education services, growth in accountability policies, increasing use of school choice programs, greater use of school district outsourcing, and increases in the number of charter schools"

(p. 11). Further, the No Child Left Behind Act allows for supplemental educational services to be delivered by outside organizations to students who do not meet the proficiency standards.

Clearly, a key feature of the diverse service provider model involves the district's willingness to grant management autonomy to the contracted service providers, which in turn agree to meet certain measurable outcomes within a given time frame. In this governance arrangement, the contracted service providers are expected to be cost efficient and raise performance levels.

There is much debate as to how outside organizations will manage schools. Proponents of the model argue that diverse providers will promote innovation and raise performance without additional financial cost to the district. There are those who see the model as a step toward "market efficiency." From this perspective then, the diverse service model creates opportunity for locally designed school improvement efforts to be offered as an alternative to the district-driven policy.

Skeptics of the model remain concerned about treating public education as a marketplace. Even though the diverse service model may attract the nonprofit sector to manage schools (such as universities and museums), there has been a noticeable growth in for-profit involvement as well. At issue is whether diverse service providers can incorporate local community values. For example, school context and educators' skepticism may pose a major challenge to any generic approach that is adopted by the organization's headquarters. To the extent that political barriers do get in the way, one would expect that the diverse providers are less likely to take risk in pushing for innovative reform, thus decreasing the opportunity for success.

With regard to the effects of the diverse service provider model on student achievement, the research findings remain largely mixed. A 2002 General Accountability Office (GAO) synthesis of studies of Edison, Mosaica, and Chancellor Beacon found that "little is known about the effectiveness of these companies' programs on student achievement, parental satisfaction, parental involvement, or school climate because few rigorous studies have been conducted" (GAO, 2002, p. 2). A year later, the GAO (2003) carried out its own achievement study, but found that "analyses of test scores in 6 cities yielded mixed results" (p. 2).

While the evidence on student achievement remains inconclusive, large urban districts seem ready to launch the diverse service provider model as a strategy to raise student performance. Philadelphia's experience with the educational management organizations (including Edison) and Chicago's Renaissance 2010 (including a whole new set of charter schools) offer two such examples. Lessons learned from these two cities will have important implications for urban school reform across the nation.

Short of contracting with an educational management organization to operate a restructured school, a district policy of including various contractual service providers for particular aspects of a school's operation is a viable option. This also enables the school's management to focus on areas of operation not provided by the contractors.

10. Create an accountability-oriented, technology-based support system

Measurable results for all students are the driving force in today's schools. To meet these challenges, districts adopt system-wide management strategies. One approach is to promote web-based portals in support of classroom instruction, curricular choices, and student assessment. Houston, for example, in response to the standards established in the Texas Assessment of Knowledge and Skills (TAKS), creates and maintains a web-based portal (HISDConnect) for teachers, principals, and administrators. The Teacher Toolbox enables teachers to use their district-purchased, individual laptop computers to access Profiler for Academic Success of Students, a comprehensive student information management system which includes model lessons for each grade and subject areas and extensive resources for professional development. Based on a web-based survey of teachers and administrators in the district, researchers found that teachers favored a combination of online tutorial and campus-based training for professional development (Brier et al., 2006; Wong et al., 2006). While high school principals relied on central office staff for technical support, elementary and middle school principals seemed more likely to utilize the web-based tutorial and data management system. Further, only 35% of the Title 1 Coordinators reported that the central office was a useful training source. Another implementation challenge was that one out of four high school principals did not utilize the online student assessment tools. Nevertheless, technology-based support systems enable a district to infuse the system with access to high-quality guidance on school improvement that is useful in stemming the need for restructuring as well as in guiding the full implementation of a restructuring plan.

References

Black, P., & Wiliam, D. (1998). Inside the black box: Raising standards through classroom assessment. *Phi Delta Kappan, 80*(2), 139-44.

Brier, B., et al. (2006). When technology supports teachers' work: Implementation of Houston's Teacher Tools Online Initiative. In K. Wong & S. Rutledge (Eds.), *System-wide efforts to improve student achievement*. Greenwich, CT: Information Age Publishing.

Bushweller, K. (2003). Education business. *Education Week, 23*(14).

Dillon, S. (2005, September 2). Education law is loosened for failing Chicago schools. *New York Times*, p. A11.

General Accountability Office. (2002). *Public schools: Insufficient research to determine effectiveness of selected private education companies.* Washington, DC: Author.

General Accountability Office. (2003). *Public schools: Comparison of achievement results for students attending privately managed and traditional schools in six cities.* Washington, DC: Author.

Marsh, J., Kerr, K., Ikemoto, G., & Darilek, H. (2006). Developing district-intermediary partnerships to promote instructional improvement: Early experiences and lessons about the institute for learning. In K. Wong & S. Rutledge, (Eds.), *System-wide efforts to improve student achievement.* Greenwich, CT: Information Age Publishing.

National School Boards Foundation. (1999). *Leadership matters: Transforming urban school boards.* Alexandria, VA: Author.

Stone, C. (2003, June 24). *Civic capacity: What, why and whence.* Unpublished manuscript.

Wong, K. (2006). The political dynamics of mayoral engagement in public education. *Harvard Educational Review, 76*(2).

Wong, K., Buice, J., & Cole, K. (2006). Integrated governance in Trenton Public Schools (NJ): Coordinated efforts to raise performance in high schools. In K. Wong & S. Rutledge (Eds.), *System-wide efforts to improve student achievement.* Greenwich, CT: Information Age Publishing.

Wong, K., et al. (2006). District initiatives to improve curriculum and instruction: Views of administrators on Houston's Teacher Tools Online Initiative. In K. Wong & S. Rutledge (Eds.), *System-wide efforts to improve student achievement.* Greenwich, CT: Information Age Publishing.

Wong, K., & Nicotera, A. (2006). Peer coaching as a strategy to build instructional capacity in low performing schools. In K. Wong & S. Rutledge (Eds.), *System-wide efforts to improve student achievement.* Greenwich, CT: Information Age Publishing.

Additional Resources

Barr, R., & Dreeben, R. (1983). *How schools work.* Chicago: University of Chicago Press.

Hall, D., Weiner, R., & Carey, K. (2003). *What new "AYP" information tells us about schools, states, and public education.* Washington, DC: The Education Trust.

Hochschild, J. (2003). Rethinking accountability politics. In P. E. Peterson & M. R. West, (Eds.), *No child left behind? The politics and practice of school accountability.* Washington, DC: The Brookings Institution Press.

King, G., Keohane, R., & Verba, S. (1994). *Designing social inquiry: Scientific inference in qualitative research.* Princeton: Princeton University Press.

McCabe, M. (2006). State of the states. *Quality Counts at 10.* Bethesda, MD: Education Week.

Roeber, E. D. (2002). *Appropriate inclusion of students with disabilities in state accountability systems.* Denver: Education Commission of the States.

Wong, K, & Nicotera, A. (2007). *Successful schools and educational accountability.* Boston: Allyn & Bacon.

About the Author

Kenneth Wong is the Walter and Leonore Annenberg Professor in Education Policy and the Director of the Urban Education Policy Program at Brown University and a member of the Center on Innovation & Improvement's Scientific Coucil. He taught at Vanderbilt University and the University of Chicago. In 2004, he was awarded a $10 million grant by the Institute of Education Sciences to establish and direct the National Center on School Choice, Competition, and Student Achievement. He is nationally known for his research in educational innovation, outcome-based accountability, and governance redesign (including charter schools, city and state takeover, and Title I schoolwide reform). He has advised the U.S. Congress, state legislatures, mayoral offices, and the leadership in several large urban school systems on how to redesign the accountability framework. He earned his PhD in Political Science from the University of Chicago in 1983.

2. The School Board and Central Office in District Improvement

Gordon Cawelti and Nancy Protheroe

Both the pace and extent of improvements in student achievement can be substantially impacted by a systemic and coherent district-wide initiative focused on instruction and supported by strong district leadership.

Abstract

An increasingly robust research base demonstrates the critical role school districts can play in school improvement and in schools' efforts to meet standards. A key element is strong leadership by a superintendent and school board willing and able to publicly recognize challenges, develop a plan for reform, and build support for needed changes. Both equity and excellence must be addressed, with the focus of reform efforts clearly centered on instruction. Districts must take the lead in establishing "no excuses" goals and in developing initiatives designed to move all schools toward these. However, it also must be clear that accountability for carrying out these initiatives – and for ensuring every student learns – is in the hands of principals and teachers. To support them and to ensure improvement efforts stay on track, districts should remain actively engaged through efforts such as creation of a curricular focus, intensive development opportunities for staff, monitoring of progress, and provision of resources needed to address intervention needs of individual students.

Handbook on Restructuring and Substantial School Improvement

Copyright © 2007 by Information Age Publishing and The Academic Development Institute

Introduction

This module summarizes research focused on the district role in improving student achievement – specifically, on practices of high-achieving school districts. Understanding and implementing the principles presented in this module are critical if the pace and extent of school improvement is to be accelerated towards the goal of all students meeting standards.

The research base about the practices of high-achieving school districts consists of case studies, with the findings thus best characterized as "best practices." (See the reference list for information on studies used.) However, the striking commonalities among the strategies identified across studies provide evidence that lessons from the studied districts' experiences can be a valuable resource for other districts engaged in reform.

Findings from the studies are also well-aligned to broad lessons already mentioned by Hassel, Hassel, and Rhim in the introduction to this *Handbook*. These were identified originally as part of a project designed to review research on restructuring across industries and so inform NCLB restructuring efforts; specifically,

- large, fast improvements are different from incremental changes over time;
- eradicating low performance is not a one-time project; it is a commitment that is a core part of school and district work; and
- district and school leaders must possess a steely will and a compass set firmly on children's learning (pp. 12-13).

Thus, while NCLB restructuring provisions focus on schools, identifying systemic ways in which districts can provide effective support for schools' improvement efforts should be an integral part of restructuring.

The phrase "high-achieving school districts" is used thoughout the module, and understanding what that means in this context is important to other districts interested in applying the lessons learned. The districts studied served populations of students typically considered to be at-risk of school failure – students from low-income families, students of color, and English language learners. Not surprisingly, the districts had not always been high-achieving. They had low pass rates on state assessments, and, for many of them, public dissatisfaction with the schools was growing. It is at that place their progress toward high student achievement began.

Strategies identified in the research are discussed here as 10 principles. In addition to these principles, the research base provides other important lessons about the district role in improvement efforts. Perhaps most important, districts can "make a difference" and, through focused effort and plain hard work, have a substantial positive impact on school improvement efforts.

Change was extensive in all the districts, and was approached systemically. All areas were affected including what was taught and how, as well as structures and roles for people across the system.

The most successful efforts were coherent and comprehensive. Each district also took on multiple initiatives, with these intended to be mutually reinforcing whenever possible. In addition, the most successful districts were more likely to limit these to a few key areas.

There was a focus on both excellence and equity. While it was obvious that low-achieving groups needed to make substantial progress, the bar was not set so low that reaching it would ultimately do students a disservice.

District leaders knew that, often, fundamental change was needed in schools and classrooms, so reform initiatives all included elements that "pushed" them to the school and classroom levels. Finally, district leadership understood that there would be no quick fixes, with leaders communicating their intention to stay the course.

The discussion of principles in this chapter summarizes findings that are common across studies. The part they played in the success stories of multiple districts highlights their potential to support improvement in other districts. However, more detailed stories of individual districts studied – available in reports included in the reference list at the end of the chapter – can be another valuable resource for school leaders.

Principles

1. Provide high expectations and focused leadership

In all the districts studied, a central theme was superintendent leadership. A superintendent's role in leveraging district policies and resources to accelerate school-level improvement was critical, with such efforts providing valuable lessons for other superintendents.

These district leaders must be skilled in both articulating direction for the district and getting others to buy into these goals, since without such buy in improvement will be lackluster at best. They must be willing to face reality and acknowledge the often daunting challenges. This is critical to building the will to change, and failing to do so can limit progress in restructuring the system for greater accountability and results.

Leadership around the goal of all students learning must be at the core of a district's efforts to improve. To provide such leadership, superintendents in particular must be relentless in their efforts to convey messages of high expectations and no excuses. This may require use of examples of high levels of learning achieved by high-risk student populations in neighboring districts or in schools and classrooms in the district's own schools.

Specific achievement targets for the district, for individual schools, and for subpopulations of students should be developed to sharpen the focus on improvement. Some of these targets may be short-term and so provide ongoing gauges of progress. Others may be lofty – for example, ensuring all students will graduate ready for college – and so provide a longer view of what the district is working toward.

The district's vision and goals should drive programmatic and financial decisions at all levels of the system. The superintendent is key to making this happen, and much of this leader's efforts must be on ensuring district goals translate into what happens in the daily life of schools and classrooms. In pragmatic terms, this means providing schools' staff with the resources, tools, and support they need, while unceasingly focusing on the need for improvement in student achievement.

Finally, research focused on high-performing districts also demonstrates the importance of the *nature* of leadership. While different styles were observed among the superintendents studied, it is the intensity of their leadership – especially in regard to communicating the message of high expectations – that is striking. These superintendents are characterized as focusing on the message with an almost missionary zeal.

2. Engage school boards and community leaders

Agreement between the board and superintendent in regard to philosophy and goals provides critical support for district improvement efforts. However, the superintendent and school board in a district facing a crisis in student achievement and public confidence should spend whatever time is needed to talk through issues in an effort to ensure the improvement initiative will be presented – and supported on an ongoing basis – with a united front.

School boards must play an active role, continuously and publicly providing support for the reform initiative through several key actions. First, the school board should engage in intensive and ongoing efforts to communicate and sell the vision for reform to the community. They should talk with community members about the plan, gather perspectives and ideas, and use these – in collaboration with the superintendent and other district leaders – to refine the plan.

On an ongoing basis, the school board should act as a monitor to ensure student learning remains the top priority for attention and resources. The question should be asked repeatedly: How will doing this – or not doing it – affect student achievement?

The school board should use its policy role to develop policies that support improvement efforts. Boards should also engage in periodic self-evaluation, asking whether they are solidly focused on this policy role, not diverted by administrative matters. However, they should still be knowledgeable about district programs and of the ways in which these contribute to overall improvement efforts. School board time and assistance from district staff will be needed to ensure board members have the opportunity to learn about programs and initiatives.

District leaders should work to engage the community – parents, business leaders, civic groups, and churches – in improvement efforts, perhaps using data about poor student performance to demonstrate the need to change and so galvanize broad-based support for district initiatives. Alternately, if players outside the district structure are taking action to jumpstart reform efforts, district leaders should work with them to identify areas of concern as well as ways all parties can work together to improve student achievement.

3. Tie results to people

Although many of the high-achieving districts studied initiated reforms as a direct result of increased accountability pressures from their states, they quickly progressed to make accountability part of the overall district culture – in clear contrast with districts making less progress. Thus, they provide an important lesson for districts engaged in broad-based improvement efforts: high expectations and "no excuses" must be accompanied by clear expectations of personal responsibility for results.

Accountability for results begins at the top in effective districts, with superintendents explicitly signaling their willingness to be held accountable. This more rigorous approach to accountability typically should begin with the development of specific goals, deadlines, and consequences, with both district- and school-level staff held responsible for producing results. For example, principals might be employed using performance contracts tied to goals. This clearly sends the message that they are responsible for leading the way in closing achievement gaps and in getting buy in from teachers.

Explicit procedures also will be needed to ensure teachers are – and feel – personally accountable for student learning. For example, through use of interim or formative testing, teachers can be kept informed about student mastery of required skills, with principals leading discussion about areas of concern and possible solutions. Using this information, teachers should be expected to adjust instruction to ensure individual students achieve mastery. This will represent a major shift for many teachers, and principals will need to provide more intensive support for low-performing or anxious teachers.

This shift in accountability to individual teachers should be accompanied by district and school initiatives that provide opportunities for teachers to work together around issues of student learning. During this time, they may, for example, develop lesson plans or analyze assessment data.

Obviously, since teachers and principals will feel the pressure of increased expectations for performance, they should also be provided with resources to help achieve them (see, for example, principles 5 and 6). Often, this requires a redefinition of the role of central office staff from oversight to support.

One approach would be to partner some central office staff members with specific schools, especially low-performing schools, for intensive work on improvement efforts. Other central office departments, such as human resources, might have their roles more explicitly defined as service providers for schools, with procedures put in place to assess school staff satisfaction with their efforts and processes.

Finally, consequences for accountability should include the potential for recognition and celebration. These serve to both affirm the possibility of improvement and energize people for future efforts.

4. Ensure local curriculum alignment with state standards

The high-performing school districts studied became more explicit about what was to be taught using skills and knowledge included on state assessments as guides, all of which resulted in more standardization across schools. While this is considered to be common practice for school districts, it was the intensity and single-mindedness with which it was done which was uncommon. The curriculum guides developed in these districts – in contrast with many others – were used continuously, not filed on shelves. This is a lesson any district engaging in reform should take seriously.

Explicit, focused efforts should be made to ensure alignment of the written, taught, and tested curricula. This process of curriculum alignment and mapping should be comprehensive and integrated across grades.

The process will require a shift in some districts from site-based decision making to more centralized direction about what will be taught. Such a shift ensures everyone – in all schools – is aiming in the same direction. It also permits district resources to be used in a more focused way. For example, intensive teacher and curriculum development can be provided on the district-wide approach to teaching reading.

In addition, this more uniform approach to instruction is likely to have disproportionately positive effects on students most at risk and greater impact in schools with greater challenges. As an example, in a district with high intra-district student mobility, the shift to a more uniform approach means that a student moving from one district school to another will be more likely to be able to pick up at close to the same spot in the curriculum.

Common practices might include intensive efforts to align content taught across grades and the development of pacing guides, with cross-district and cross-grade teams of teachers assigned to work on these tasks. Teachers in districts studied who participated in such work groups reported having a much clearer idea of what was taught in prior grades – as well as the academic expectations for their own. Opportunities to work together also helped them to feel both more professional and more personally invested in their districts' reform efforts.

In addition to pacing guides and sample lessons, districts should consider developing networks of instructional experts, such as mentor teachers or content area specialists working in the central office, to support teachers as they begin to teach the "new" curriculum. Finally, district leaders should put in place mechanisms – for example, requiring principals to spend more time in classrooms – to monitor whether the intended curriculum is actually being taught.

5. Reallocate resources to better support goals and programs

High-performing school districts allocate financial and human resources strategically to support their goals of improving instruction and so student achievement. This requires a conscious and highly intentional shift away from allowing year-to-year changes in resource levels to determine the program to having clearly articulated, goal-based needs govern the budgeting process.

The reallocations also should provide concrete indicators of other principles described here. For example, districts typically will need to provide special support to assist students with academic difficulties by funding after-school programs or other intervention programs. Both excellence and equity issues must be addressed. This would include such strategies as providing schools with especially needy populations with special funding for lower pupil-teacher ratios for basic skills instruction.

More than financial resources will need to be reallocated. A typical and important shift in the high-performing districts was in their use of time. Districts – and schools with district encouragement – will need to invest heavily in the use of teacher and other staff time to support instruction by, for example, engaging in efforts to analyze assessment data or realigning class loads to create time for a master teacher to work with other teachers.

Staff development will need to receive an often significant increase in resources. It must also become more intentional, with teacher development strategically aligned with initiatives embedded in the district's improvement effort. Development opportunities for principals also should be considered a critical piece of improvement efforts. This might include approaches such as training in data use as well as opportunities for principals to meet together for discussions about common issues.

Resource reallocation also will need to be done at the school level, with districts providing this flexibility. For example, some schools may need to shift teaching positions to allow a teacher to work at least part-time as the school data coordinator.

With finances in many districts already stretched, the process of allocating resources often will be difficult. There will be "costs" in terms of programs receiving decreased emphasis. Districts will need to consider trade-offs and implications strategically. In addition, they should work toward efficient use of all available funds. This may include approaches such as becoming more intentional and creative in the use of categorical funds, perhaps pooling them to fund desired initiatives.

6. Use data to drive decisions

Data-based decision making has been discussed so often by educators in recent years it seems almost unnecessary to name it as one of the ten principles discussed here. However, it was identified across studies as a key element of reform efforts, with the districts embedding data use in improvement efforts and used as an important lever for change. Decisions were no longer made on instinct, and data was required to justify decisions about programs and resources.

In addition, data was used to monitor progress and ensure attention stayed on instructional goals. In the words of a superintendent from a studied district, "If we don't maintain the focus by using the assessment data, the events of the day will take precedence over school improvement issues" (Donicht, in Cawelti & Protheroe, 2001, p. 46). In the high-achieving districts, effective use of data contributed to improvement efforts at the district, school, and classroom levels.

Districts working to increase productive use of data should take into account three important elements. First, data use should focus primarily on issues of student learning. Second, systems must be developed to ensure key pieces of *user-friendly* data are available *in a timely fashion* at the district, school, and classroom levels. Third, staff members will need training in how to use data as well as time to analyze it, discuss it, and use it on a routine basis to adjust instruction to better meet students' needs.

A district's use of data – if done well – will become qualitatively different and more sophisticated over time. While a typical first step is use of data from annual assessments, districts should move toward use of interim and diagnostic mini-assessments to monitor student progress on a continuing basis. These assessments might be developed by teacher teams at the district or school level, or obtained through an external source. The key to their value is use at the teacher, school, and district levels to identify needs of individual students, weak areas of the curriculum or instruction, or strategic efforts requiring additional resources.

Although the initial focus will be on achievement measures, additional indicators – such as attendance rates and parent satisfaction – should also become part of the data package. Districts should also consider defining data more broadly than simply numbers collected through assessments or surveys. For example, Learning Walks – in which a team of teachers, principals, and central office staff visits classrooms and then discuss observations – could be used to monitor use of curriculum guides by teachers. Finally, districts working to increase their use of data will find they need to develop an infrastructure to collect, analyze, and ensure effective use of data.

7. Intervene in schools making little progress

Although all the principles discussed in this module have implications for districts working to improve individual schools, this principle has the most direct connection to NCLB restructuring requirements, specifically that "significant changes" may need to be made in the school's staffing and governance. Because it is clear schools serving large numbers of children from low-income families or facing other challenges can be very successful in ensuring all or most students achieve high standards, district policies and practices should begin with the assumption that a turnaround is indeed possible. The challenge of improving a low-performing school is especially important from the perspective of equity since it is more likely that children at greater risk due to familial factors will be enrolled in such schools.

The problem of low-performing schools is also clearly a district responsibility. Therefore, districts should have well-developed and communicated policies and procedures in regard to them as an integral part of the reform initiative.

Drawing from research on high-performing organizations in the corporate world, a district would begin by having the right people in place in a significantly underperforming school *before* major restructuring efforts are undertaken. This might include efforts such as staff reassignments or the development and use of "turnaround principals."

Plans for school improvement efforts should include benchmarks and timelines as well as more general goals, with explicit consequences identified for not meeting benchmarks. The message also needs to be clear in regard to expectations for what will be taught and when, if these have been established by the district.

The relationship of the district with a low-performing school should be different – tighter – from that with other schools. The low-performing school will require more attention from central office staff to provide support and monitor school efforts. Assistance provided might include, for example, helping school staff diagnose and address problems or temporarily assigning a subject area specialist to the school to work with teaching staff. The monitoring should be ongoing and might include review of data from periodic assessments, site visits, and coaches assigned to the school.

In addition, such schools may need additional resources for functions such as after-school tutoring or salary incentives for particularly effective teachers who accept reassignment to such schools. Another possibility might be a "waiver" from a district policy, for example, one that makes it easier for a principal to move a teacher out of the school.

Finally, a district should consider developing a system of incentives alongside potential sanctions. For example, a low-performing school might be given a specified period to improve. Improvement within this time would result in loosening of central office control on the school.

8. Focus teachers on student learning

Studies of high-performing school districts highlight the key to raising student achievement: improvement must begin in the classroom. By working to get research-based teaching strategies shown to be effective into every classroom, districts make use of a powerful lever for improvement.

Central office leaders can play a pivotal role in developing a strong staff development program that provides high quality training to expand the teachers' instructional repertoires. Three aspects of such development should be addressed. First, most development opportunities should be linked to district initiatives – working to educate teachers in depth on one or two topics in contrast to a scatter-gun approach. Choices about staff development topics and formats should be informed on an ongoing basis by student achievement results. This helps focus teacher efforts on key areas of concerns on an ongoing basis. In addition, it is more likely teachers will view development opportunities as relevant and responsive to their needs.

Second, the research base about "good teaching" should be mined and used. For example, a teach-assess-re-teach cycle that uses periodic formative assessment to gauge mastery, then re-teaches as necessary, is good teaching. However, teachers may need help in developing effective ways to differentiate instruction based on the results of the mini-assessments.

Third, the definition of staff development should be expanded to include such things as in-class coaching, group lesson planning, and analysis of student work. Profiles of the high-performing districts demonstrated just how powerful approaches such as this can be to improving teaching. For example, many of the districts included teachers in efforts to align curriculum and instruction to standards. Out of these efforts came explicit guides to what was to be taught and when. Teacher collaboration needed to develop the materials had an important additional benefit. Teaching moved from a closed door experience to one characterized by higher levels of collaboration and sharing of ideas.

While assuming major responsibility for teacher development, the district should make it clear that schools should also address their own unique needs – although still in ways that focus on district goals and initiatives. Finally, to provide additional support for teachers, principals should be trained in clinical supervision techniques to provide focused feedback for teachers working to improve their skills. Districts should also provide training for principals to help them work with teachers to improve instruction through conversations informed by data.

9. Assist students with academic difficulties

Clear district expectations that students meet standards must be accompanied by efforts to help students falling behind. While this is likely a part of every district's efforts, the approach used in the high-performing districts was characterized by an especially tight alignment between intervention and other aspects of the instructional process. In addition, the emphasis was on ensuring students were not left so far behind that they could never catch up. Thus, they provide clear lessons for other districts.

Efforts typically began with the recognition that waiting for data from the state assessment program would not allow for timely intervention. To address this problem, districts moved forward with the development and administration of periodic benchmark assessments, analysis of results to establish instructional needs, and provision of special services to students who needed them.

Districts supported the development of these processes through training of teachers and other staff in ways to generate and use data. Frequent formative and diagnostic mini-assessments allowed teachers to identify which students had – or had not – mastered content. In one district, a teacher-developed approach to monitoring student progress and addressing needs identified became a central focus for school improvement. This process included decision points at which students were provided with additional instructional opportunities if mastery was not achieved.

Another district developed an ongoing system in the elementary schools intended to provide students with practice as they worked to mastery on math concepts. The practice sheets were then used by teachers to gauge the progress of individual students.

Depending on their level of need, students were provided with a range of interventions. Some of these were substantial, such as after-school or summer school programs. Others happened on a more fluid basis. For example, in one middle school, teachers of each team of 150 students discussed students on their team almost daily and reshuffled students to provide 30 minutes of tutorial time focused on students' individual instructional needs.

Sometimes district support for these approaches was financial. For example, some districts funded district-wide initiatives for extended day programs for students falling behind. Sometimes, additional financial support was allocated to schools, with schools selecting options such as a computer-based package to provide struggling students with more opportunities for reading practice. District support was also embedded in projects such as the development of mini-assessments that required teacher time – but which provided timely data for use in assessing student needs on an ongoing basis.

10. Spread leadership to the school level

A challenge of district-based reform with clear expectations for school- and classroom-level accountability is developing a balance between district control and flexibility needed at the school level. Such flexibility also requires explicit efforts to "spread" leadership and build leadership skills in school staff.

High-performing school districts recognized that culture as well as processes might need to change to build leadership capacity at the school level. By demonstrating that everyone's ideas are valued, central office staff stimulates the development of potentially helpful approaches and suggestions.

This may come about through district initiatives such as curriculum alignment efforts. By providing opportunities for teachers to work together and then using the products they develop in very public ways, the leadership base begins to broaden. In addition, participation helps teachers develop skills in areas such as group processes that can be taken back to their schools and used to strengthen school improvement efforts.

This principle is also inextricably tied to strong central office leadership. Spreading leadership to the school level must begin with selling the vision of high expectations for student achievement. Principals in high-performing districts talked of coming to the realization that the ultimately successful improvement effort – in contrast with those they had experienced before – was not a case of "this too shall pass." This level of buy in is an integral part of efforts to spread leadership to the school level.

Another key element is the development of a clear understanding of district expectations for schools – as well as the parameters of school autonomy. While the focus of school efforts toward district goals must be nonnegotiable, each district will need to determine and clearly communicate to school personnel the types of decisions they are authorized to make about resource allocation and staff assignments. These parameters may be different in different districts.

In addition, a district may decide to provide more latitude for schools demonstrating high or improving student achievement than for those making little to no progress.

A critical point – school staff cannot be expected to engage in improvement efforts that may substantially change their daily work lives without support. Helping staff members, especially teachers, acquire needed skills creates an important spiral effect. They are better able to fill their newly defined roles – and with success comes increased confidence and willingness to move outside a closed-door model toward increased participation in school- and district-level improvement efforts.

To do this, districts will likely find they need to shift central office staff responsibilities from oversight to providing much needed expertise directly to schools. Central office staff will also need to work at a macro level to increase staff effectiveness. An example might be the identification of "best practices" already in use in a school or classroom, followed by the development of a process to extend use of such practices elsewhere in the district.

Summary

The message from studies of high-performing districts discussed here is clear: Systemic district-based efforts can effectively support improvement across schools. The principles discussed here also have special relevance for district efforts to turn around low-performing schools. Clearly, even major school-based restructuring efforts such as those required by NCLB are likely to be more successful in the context of an effective district.

Strong superintendent leadership, supported by a knowledgeable and collaborative school board, is key to such reform efforts. The press to reach high levels of achievement must begin with the development and communication of goals focused on high student achievement. It must also be clear that personal accountability for results is an expectation across the system, with standards, ways to monitor, and consequences in place.

Curriculum and instruction must be addressed comprehensively, with a clear plan for what will be taught. More than ever, teachers will need help to expand their repertoire of instructional strategies as they work to ensure all students make needed progress toward these instructional goals. Systems must be present to measure student progress on a continuing basis, with interventions ready to address some students' needs for additional instruction.

While the principles discussed above stress the possibilities, districts working to apply these research-based lessons about "what works" should also take heed of problems the high-achieving districts experienced.

For example, maintaining a balance between comprehensiveness and a focus on key initiatives is critical. It is also important that districts keep staff and institutional capacity in mind. Finally, in districts used to site-based management, a more structured, top-down approach – especially related to what should be taught, how, and when – may generate frustration and resistance among school staff members. Schools may also be concerned that increased standardization makes it more difficult for them to address the unique needs of their students.

But again, it is important to emphasize that success is achievable. Success in meeting high academic standards – for every student – is the key to a better life for today's youth, and research on high-performing school districts offers realistic hope for meeting this goal. By incorporating the principles discussed here in reform efforts, school districts can act as a critical lever for accelerating the pace of school improvement.

References

Anderson, S. A. (2003). *The district role in educational change: A review of the literature.* Toronto, ON: International Centre for Educational Change, Ontario Institute for Studies in Education. Retrieved Fall 2006 from http://fcis.oise.utoronto.ca/~icec/workpaper2.pdf

Cawelti, G., & Protheroe, N. (2001). *High student achievement: How six school districts changed into high-performance systems.* Arlington, VA: Educational Research Service.

Dailey, D., Fleischman, S., Gil, L., Holtzman, D., O'Day, J., & Vosmer, C. (2005). *Toward more effective school districts: A review of the knowledge base.* Washington, DC: American Institutes for Research. Retrieved Fall 2006 from http://www.air.org/projects/Toward%20More%20Effective%20Scchool%20Districts-A%20Review%20of%20the%20Knowledge%20Base%206-14-05%20313%20pm.pdf

Fouts, J. T. (2003). *A decade of reform: A summary of research findings on classroom, school, and district effectiveness in Washington state.* Lynwood, WA: Washington School Research Center. Retrieved Fall 2006 from http://www.spu.edu/wsrc/ADecadeofReformOctober192003v5.pdf

Iowa Association of School Boards. (2001, Winter). School boards and student achievement: A comparison of governance in high-and low-achieving districts. *ERS Spectrum*, 38-46.

Kercheval, A, & Newbill, S. L. (2002). *A case study of key effective practices in Ohio's improved school districts.* Bloomington, IN: Indiana Center for Evaluation. Retrieved Fall 2006 from http://www.indiana.edu/~ceep/projects/PDF/200107_Key_Effec_Prac_Interim_Report.pdf

Maguire, P. (2003). *District practices and student achievement: Lessons from Alberta.* Kelowna, BC: Society for the Advancement of Excellence in Education. Retrieved Fall 2006 from http://www.saee.ca/publications/A_019_BBI_MID.php

Massell, D. (2000). *The district role in building capacity: Four strategies* (Policy Briefs). Philadelphia: Consortium for Policy Research in Education, University of Pennsylvania. Retrieved Fall 2006 from http://www.cpre.org/Publications/rb32.pdf

McLaughlin, M., & Talbert, J. (2003). *Reforming districts: How districts support school reform.* Seattle: Center for the Study of Teaching and Policy, University of Washington. Retrieved Fall 2006 from http://depts.washington.edu/ctpmail/PDFs/ReformingDistricts-09-2003.pdf

McLaughlin, M. W., Talbert, J. E., Gilbert, S., Hightower, A. M., Husbands, J. L., Marsh, J. A., & Young, V. M. (2004). *Districts as change agents: Levers for system-wide instructional improvement.* Center for the Study of Teaching and Policy. Paper presented at the Annual Meeting of the American Educational Research Association, San Diego, CA.

Petrides, L., & Nodine, T. (2005). *Anatomy of school system improvement: Performance-driven practices in urban school districts.* San Francisco: New Schools Venture Fund. Retrieved Fall 2006 from http://www.newschools.org/viewpoints/documents/District_Performance_Practices.pdf

Public Schools of North Carolina. (2000). *Improving student performance: The role of district-level staff* (Evaluation Brief). Retrieved Fall 2006 from http://www.ncpublicschools.org/docs/accountability/evaluation/evalbriefs/vol2n4-role.pdf

Shannon, G. S., & Bylsma, P. (2004). *Characteristics of improved school districts: Themes from research.* Olympia, WA: Office of Superintendent of Public Instruction. Retrieved Fall 2006 from http://www.k12.wa.us/research/pubdocs/DistrictImprovementReport.pdf

Skrla, L., Scheurich, J., & Johnson, J., Jr. (2000). *Equity-driven achievement-focused school districts: A report on systemic school success in four Texas school districts serving diverse student populations.* Austin: The Charles A. Dana Center, The University of Texas at Austin.

Snipes, J., Doolittle, F., & Herlihy, C. (2002). *Foundations for success: Case studies of how urban school systems improve student achievement.* Washington, DC: MDRC for the Council of the Great City Schools. Retrieved Fall 2006 from http://www.mdrc.org/publications/47/full.pdf

Standard & Poor's. (2006). *Kansas Education Resource Management Study – Phase III: A synthesis of highly resource-effective district strategies.* New York: Author. Retrieved Fall 2006 from http://www.schoolmatters.com/pdf/special_reports/Ks/District_Strategies.pdf

Togneri, W., & Anderson, S. E. (2003). *Beyond islands of excellence: What districts do to improve instruction and achievement in all schools.* Alexandria, VA: Learning First Alliance. Retrieved Fall 2006 from http://www.learningfirst.org/publications/districts/

Waters. J. T., & Marzano, R. J. (2006). *School district leadership that works: The effect of superintendent leadership on student achievement* (Working Paper). Denver, CO: Mid-continent Research for Education and Learning. Retrieved Fall 2006 from http://www.mcrel.org/pdf/leadershiporganizationdevelopment/4005RR_Superintendent_Leadership.pdf

About the Authors

Gordon Cawelti served from 1992 to 2006 as Senior Research Associate for the Educational Research Service (ERS) in Arlington, VA, and a member of the Center on Innovation & Improvement's Scientific Council. While at ERS, he conducted research on various approaches to improving student achievement, with the most recent focus a study of high-performing districts. He also served as Director of The Achievement Consortium which was sponsored by the Mid-Atlantic Regional Educational Laboratory. He received his PhD from the University of Iowa, served as a science teacher and a high school principal, and as Executive Director of the North Central Association in Chicago. From 1969-1973 he served as superintendent of the Tulsa Public School District where he was involved in developing several innovative schools, undertook an extensive school construction program, and provided leadership in the school desegregation process which eliminated all racially isolated schools. In Washington he served for 19 years as Executive Director of the Association for Supervision and Curriculum Development. He has served as a management consultant to many school districts in the areas of instructional leadership, school restructuring, and improving student achievement, and has provided training in several countries in the Middle East, Europe, and the Far East. He conducted one of the first national studies of high-performing school districts.

Nancy Protheroe is the director of special research projects at Educational Research Service (ERS) and a member of the Center on Innovation & Improvement's Scientific Council. She is responsible for projects such as the *Informed Educator* series, the ERS *What We Know About* reports, the *Essentials for Principals* series published with the National Association of Elementary School Principals, and the *Supporting Good Teaching* series. In addition, she was the co-director of a federally funded Transition to Teaching program that prepared alternative route teachers for positions in special education. While at ERS, she has managed the development and production of a variety of products intended to analyze and summarize research and practice on critical issues for use by school personnel. A topical emphasis over the past decade has been school- and district-level efforts to improve student achievement, and in collaboration with Gordon Cawelti, conducted a study of high-achieving school districts. She also has developed and conducted workshops for school personnel on use of research to raise student achievement, effective use of data in decision making, and needs assessment techniques for schools and school districts. She received her M.Ed. in Educational Administration and Student Services from Kent State University, Kent, OH. She conducted one of the first national studies of high-performing school districts.

3. Restructuring Options and Change Processes

Carole L. Perlman

In selecting an NCLB restructuring option, employ data, evidence-based practices, and knowledge of the change process.

Abstract

Successful restructuring under NCLB requires dramatic change in a short period of time; an understanding of the change process can smooth the way. It will be necessary to carefully assess each school's strengths and needs and to use the resulting data to select an appropriate restructuring option and craft a plan that includes strategic allocation of available resources and reliance on evidence-based improvement models. Collaborative support from the district is essential for school restructuring to succeed.

Introduction

Under the federal No Child Left Behind Act (NCLB), schools that do not make Adequate Yearly Progress (AYP) for five consecutive years are required to develop plans for "restructuring" in the sixth year. If they fail to make AYP in Year 6, they must implement their restructuring plans in Year 7. NCLB provides five options for schools in restructuring to follow:

1. reopen the school as a public charter school;
2. replace "all or most of the school staff (which may include the principal) who are relevant to the failure to make adequate yearly progress";

Handbook on Restructuring and Substantial School Improvement

Copyright © 2007 by Information Age Publishing and The Academic Development Institute

3. contract with an outside "entity, such as a private management company, with a demonstrated record of effectiveness, to operate the public school";

4. turn the "operation of the school over to the State educational agency, if permitted under State law and agreed to by the State"; or

5. engage in another form of major restructuring that makes fundamental reforms, "such as significant changes in the school's staffing and governance, to improve student academic achievement in the school and that has substantial promise of enabling the school to make adequate yearly progress."(No Child Left Behind, Sec. 1116, 20, U.S.C.A. §6301-6578, 2002)

Successful restructuring requires dramatic change in a short period of time. The purpose of this chapter is to explain the change process, discuss the restructuring options offered under NCLB, and explore some ways districts can support restructuring schools. Most of all, the purpose of the chapter is to introduce you to some outstanding resources. Chief among them is the *School Restructuring Under No Child Left Behind: What Works When? A Guide for Education Leaders* (Hassel et al., 2006), which contains a multitude of helpful tools and suggestions. Although research on NCLB restructuring is in its infancy, research from other disciplines on change and turnarounds can offer valuable insights, as can research on the Comprehensive School Reform Program.

Principles

1. Prepare for change

At its heart, restructuring is a change process. It requires substantial organizational transformations that differ from the minor, incremental changes that suffice to help already good schools improve.

The literature on school change (e.g., Hassel et al., 2006; ADI, n.d.; Reinventing Education, 2002) suggests that the following are necessary for needed changes to be successful:

- A clear vision. What will the school look like when the restructuring process is completed?

- An empowered leader, a change agent, who can maintain a focus on the vision, motivate members of the school community, plan, communicate, and persist in keeping the change process on track. Getting the right leader in each school and the right oversight by the district are critical.

- Improvement teams, generally at both the district and school level. These teams, which should have no more than seven or eight members, work with the team leader to create improvement plans and obtain input from and communicate with all members of the school community. District teams' decisions can be informed by input from the school teams.

- Involvement of the whole school community: faculty, support staff, parents, community members, and students; in particular, soliciting input and keeping lines of communication open.
- Sufficient time to craft a quality plan. A summer is not enough.
- Small, "quick wins." Relatively small, simple changes that have large, quick payoffs. These provide the momentum for more difficult changes.

It will come as no surprise that change will be difficult and not everyone will happily climb aboard, even if the final goal is to provide the students with a better education. Involving some of the skeptics in improvement teams and keeping formal and informal lines of communication open can help reduce resistance. So can the results of the "quick wins." Nonetheless, it is probably less productive to focus on the naysayers than to provide support and encouragement to the willing, who can then serve as role models for the others. Another helpful tactic involves using informal relationships to get a few influential members of the school community to commit themselves to the change process and bring others with them.

It will often be the case that schools in restructuring have been the target of previous improvement efforts. Examining the results of these efforts can prove enlightening. Do any elements of the change remain? What aspects worked? Which did not? Why? How did the faculty react to the changes?

District and school staff should understand that things may well get worse before they get better. Many change processes are characterized by an initial, optimistic "honeymoon" period, followed by a second phase, in which enthusiasm is replaced by pessimism and declining morale as problems surface and resistance increases. If the leaders persist in supporting the change process, there can be a rebound as positive results appear and confidence returns. It is also true that many restructuring efforts, no matter how well-conceived, will fail. Sometimes repeated restructuring will be necessary.

Hassel et al. provide useful tools to begin the change process and get planning teams started. Another excellent set of tools for planning and managing the change process is the web-based Reinventing Change Toolkit, www.reinventingeducation.org, the result of a collaboration by IBM, the Council of Chief State School Officers, the National Association of Elementary School Principals, and the National Association of Secondary School Principals. Based on the work of Rosabeth Moss Kanter, it provides explanations of the various aspects of change and change leadership, diagnostic tools that automatically yield summary data, real-life vignettes, videos, and advice. Included in the Toolkit are sections on conceptualizing the change process and leading change. Some sample topics are "Enlisting Supporters: Getting Buy-In and

Building Coalitions," "Changing Organizational Culture and Character," and "Designing and Planning Change Projects." The Toolkit's school improvement section covers learning alignment, data-driven decision-making, quality teaching, and parental support. Registration is required, but free, and includes the capability to track your own projects.

2. Assess each school's strengths and needs

The decision on which restructuring path to take should be based on a systematic and thorough assessment of the school's strengths and weaknesses. The data obtained will form a sound basis for subsequent decisions and plans. Be sure to pay particular attention to any subgroups of students that are not making Adequate Yearly Progress.

Although a school is placed in restructuring based on state assessment results and other criteria determined by the state, consider what other data sources are available, including other formative and summative assessments given to your students, attendance, graduation, and promotion data, and results of surveys of teachers, students, and parents. The planning team should decide what data to collect and why. Look at several years' worth of data if possible. What trends do you see? Are students almost always performing well in some areas and poorly in others? Are some groups consistently performing better than others? Is your school just barely failing to make AYP or is it significantly below? Are just a few subgroups failing to make AYP, or is the school as a whole?

There are many needs assessment formats from which to choose. Some states have created their own; for example, the California Department of Education has the Academic Program Survey for schools and the District Assistance Survey, which enables districts to assess the level of support they provide their schools (Center on Education Policy, 2006). An additional survey, the Least Restrictive Environment Self Assessment, was designed to help schools examine the educational opportunities afforded students with disabilities.

Fox (2005) provides a framework for analyzing how various aspects of school governance – organization, systems, policies, procedures, practices, and personnel – affect students' AYP. Though this framework is specifically aimed at schools in Year 4 of Program Improvement, Fox's methodology could benefit others as well.

The National Center for Educational Accountability (NCEA), a collaborative effort of the University of Texas at Austin, the Education Commission of the States, and Just for the Kids, provides a self-audit, the Best Practice Framework, (http://www.just4kids.org/bestpractice/self_audit_framework.cfm?sub=tools) that enables district and school staff to compare their instructional and organizational practices with those of consistently higher-performing schools and districts. The self-audit is also designed to diagnose issues of communication and policy implementation. Five questionnaires are available for district staff and ten for schools. Survey results can be completed online and results compiled automatically or questionnaires may be printed and tabulated by hand. The Framework includes:

- Curriculum and Academic Goals
- Staff Selection, Leadership, and Capacity Building
- Instructional Programs, Practices, and Arrangements
- Monitoring: Compilation, Analysis and Use of Data Recognition, Intervention, and Adjustment

The site also offers case studies of successful schools in 20 states that illustrate best practice in each of the framework elements.

The Reinventing Education website cited in the previous section contains a host of diagnostic instruments; links are at http://www.reinventingeducation. org/RE3Web/ctk?BrowseTools&action=OPEN_INDEX&view=1 (free registration is required).

3. Weigh the alternatives: NCLB restructuring options

Five options are available to restructuring schools:

1. Reopening the school as a public charter school (subject to state law)
2. Turning over management of the school to an outside entity
3. Turnaround, i.e., replacing some or all of the school staff deemed relevant to the school's failure to make AYP
4. Turning over management of the school to the state (with the state's permission and subject to state law)
5. Other major changes in governance that have substantial promise of helping students make AYP.

The U.S. Department of Education (2006) further defines this fifth "other" option to include reforms such as:

- changing the governance structure of the school to either diminish school-based management and decision making or increase control, monitoring, and oversight by the local educational agency (LEA);
- closing the school and reopening it as a focus or theme school with new staff or staff skilled in the focus area;
- reconstituting the school into smaller autonomous learning communities;
- dissolving the school and assigning students to other schools in the district;
- pairing the school in restructuring with a higher performing school; or
- expanding or narrowing the grades served (U.S. Department of Education, 2006).

Hassel et al. note that research suggests that successful restructuring will generally require a new principal, most likely from outside the school. They caution districts against the tendency to promote the assistant principal on the grounds that the assistant principal is already familiar with the school.

The types of resources available will restrict the range of options for any given school. Does the state have legislation authorizing charter schools? Are enough good charter school providers available? Do collective bargaining agreements limit staff replacement? Are enough turnaround leaders available? Are enough teachers available? What will happen to displaced staff? Are there high quality management companies and charter providers with a record of success in similar schools? Does the district have the capacity to contract with and monitor charters and external management companies? To which options is the community most open? Does the state have resources to operate the school? Is there time to prepare requests for proposals or apply for charters? Hassel et al. write that although research suggests that about 70% of turnarounds fail, turnarounds and fresh starts (closing a school and reopening it as a charter or contract school) nonetheless show the most promise in changing a poor school into a very good one quickly.

So far, "other" is the most widely adopted model (Hassel et al.). They suggest it might work best if dramatic changes are needed only for a small subgroup of students, if a school is already making some progress, and if the current principal can be trained to become a turnaround leader.

The authors provide a series of helpful tools for planning the decision-making process and deciding among the various options. They point out that "research and experience indicate that the *process* of choosing a restructuring strategy rivals the strategy itself in importance for successful change" (p. 36). They advocate getting input from school staff and parents as a way to make better decisions and reduce resistance to change. They caution, however, against letting stakeholders control the process.

4. Develop a plan

Links to your state's school improvement planning models are available at http://www.centerii.org/centerIIPublic/criteria.aspx. Click on your state and select "School and District Improvement" from the drop-down box. Additional state resources for schools in restructuring can be found by selecting "Restructuring" from the drop-down box.

There are two parts in a planning process. The first is the decision on governance, which is made by the district, preferably with substantial input from the school. The second is the school improvement planning that will likely be carried out by the school with assistance and oversight from the district.

There is no shortage of advice on how to develop school improvement plans, but some guidance on what *not* to do might be even more illuminating. The Center for Comprehensive School Reform and Improvement (2006) cited several common mistakes in the school improvement planning process:

- "An improvement planning team with the wrong members and usually too many of them" (p. 1). The solution is to find six to eight members representing various constituencies who are willing to work collaboratively.

- "The 'Everything but the Kitchen Sink' school improvement plan…. More is not necessarily better when it comes to planning. Written goals and corresponding objectives should be SMART; that is, *specific* (clear and explicit), *measurable* (so that anyone can determine if the goal has been accomplished), *attainable* (realistic and within the school's span of control), *relevant* (directly related to identified need), and *time-bound* (with a beginning, interim benchmarks, and an end)" (p. 3). The number of goals should not exceed the school's capacity to implement and monitor them.

- "Creating a plan that is celebrated at the beginning, reviewed at the end – and left in a drawer in between….Build in ongoing evaluation to facilitate continuous planning….In school improvement plans, the completion of each of these short-term evaluation cycles offers an opportunity to revisit goals, adjust strategies, and check for student progress. Effective planners build in these cycles as the plan is being written…" (p. 3).

Schmoker (2004) argues that most school improvement plans have too many goals, initiatives, and projects, with "initiatives not thoughtfully vetted on the basis of their direct or proven impact on outcomes" (p. 427). He is critical of plans that deal too little with what goes on in classrooms and operate on the assumption "that the most vital, high-leverage thinking is done primarily by 'planners' before the school year begins, rather than by teaching practitioners *throughout* the school year" (p. 427). Schmoker contends that there should be a small number of coherent goals relating to classroom instruction that are simple, measurable statements linked to student assessments. He recommends that "teams of teachers implement, assess, and adjust instruction in short-term cycles of improvement – not annually, but continuously...Our plans, our 'systemic reform' should focus primarily on establishing and sustaining the structure for just such norms of continuous improvement" (p. 427).

5. Allocate resources strategically

All of a school's resources – financial, human, time, material – should be aligned to support the school's instructional priorities. The Center for Comprehensive School Reform and Improvement (CSRI) provides advice on resource allocation and helpful planning forms for schools at http://www.centerforcsri. org/pubs/reallocation/index.html. They articulate six guiding principles:

1. Use staff efficiently and be consistent with the priorities in the school improvement plan.
2. Consider time as the most expensive resource.
3. Use community resources when possible.
4. Devote resources to the prevention of academic problems, rather than to remediation.
5. Organize instructional time to support the school's instructional focus.
6. Incorporate time for professional development and teacher collaboration into the school's daily schedule.

Mid-continent Research for Education and Learning (2003) provided the following table to assess the adequacy of school resource allocation (p. 3). The actions described in the right-hand column are more likely to result in sustained improvement.

Least Effective	Somewhat Effective	Most Effetive
Financial Resources		
The school makes some decisions about how to allocate funds in support of school improvement goals. Staff members seek new sources of funding or other support only as necessary.	The school has control over a portion of its budget. Some funds from different sources are combined and directed in support of the school's goals. Staff members regularly seek new sources of funding and other support in order to supplement existing resources.	The school has control over the majority of its budget. To the extent possible, all funds from different sources are combined and directed in support of the school's goals. Staff members actively and systematically seek new funding sources and partnerships with businesses and community organizations. Resources, including current partnerships, are regularly reviewed and evaluated to ensure that they are used in an efficient manner.
Human Resources		
Staff positions are a mix of academic, non-instructional, and specialized positions, which may not efficiently support school improvement goals and priorities.	The majority of staff positions are focused on full-time instruction and areas that fall under the school's academic goals and priorities.	All staff positions are focused on full-time instruction and areas that fall under the school's academic goals and priorities. Adult–student ratios may change depending on the specific academic area and related goals. Retention strategies are designed to minimize staff turnover.
Time and Scheduling		
Common planning or professional development events are not part of school scheduling. They rarely take place during the school day.	School schedules are arranged to provide some job-embedded, common planning time and time for professional development.	School schedules are arranged to provide appropriate time for job-embedded common planning and professional development. Class length varies to provide students with more time for meaningful instruction in core academics.

6. Establish charter schools with care

Charter schools are autonomous public schools established under charters authorized by a school district, university, or state board of education in accord with state law. A charter is a legal agreement between the authorizer and the charter holder that delineates the charter school's goals, organization, funding, and accountability. Charter schools enjoy freedom from many district and state regulations that allows them flexibility in such areas as teacher hiring and firing, assessments, curriculum materials, and length of the school day and year. As of early 2006, 40 states had legislation authorizing charter schools.

Hassel et al. (2006) contains much valuable material on charter schools, including materials to help schools decide if charters are appropriate given their circumstances. They point out that it can be the easiest way for a district to delegate school management to an external provider, but only if your state has a good charter law (a checklist for evaluating a state's charter law is included).

Hassel et al. (2006) cite a number of factors that can determine how successful a charter school will be. Among them are:

- A fair, rigorous selection process
- District staff and other resources devoted solely to authorizing and monitoring charters; those evaluating the plans must have educational, legal, and financial expertise
- A reasonable timetable for recruiting providers, planning, and organizing schools
- Community engagement
- A balance of accountability for results, support for schools, and freedom to do things differently
- A well-functioning, effective governing board
- An effective school leader with entrepreneurial traits (e.g., setting high goals, taking initiative, persistence, using data to identify and tackle weaknesses, confidence, and the ability to influence others)
- Skilled, committed staff who support the school's mission
- A caring environment for staff and students
- Internal accountability

Other excellent sources of information on charter schools are the National Association of Charter School Authorizers (www.charterauthorizers.org) and the National Alliance for Public Charter Schools (www.publiccharters.org).

7. Be proactive in dealing with contractors

There are many situations in which a school district or state may find it advantageous to engage the services of an education contractor: in establishing charter schools, management of schools in restructuring, school turnarounds, curriculum development, delivery of professional development, and supplemental education services. Such endeavors can involve substantial expenditures over a long period of time and as with any investment, an investigation into the financial soundness of the contractor is clearly in order. Will this be a sound investment? Can the contractor provide the level of service you need?

The Comprehensive School Reform Quality Center and The Finance Project (2006) provide easy-to-use tools for assessing financial viability and organizational capacity. They describe how to obtain information, list questions to ask, tell what to look for, and identify some "red flags," to which prospective customers should pay close attention. They also provide advice on how to conduct interviews with prospective contractors.

No one can guarantee a trouble-free relationship with your contractor, but some care at the start can help you avoid being diverted from the task of improving student achievement. After narrowing your choice to a small number of contractors that appear to be a good fit with your needs, it is time to learn more about the contractors as business entities. The amount of time and effort you devote to vetting potential contractors' financial and organizational health should be proportional to the expenditure and the length of time you would be working with them; short-term, low-budget projects would not generally demand the same scrutiny that would be appropriate for more expensive, long-term projects.

Three aspects of the contractor's financial viability include its financial management system, financial stability, and funding diversity and sustainability. The measure of the quality of its financial management system is a history of "clean" audits performed by an external auditor. Financially stable contractors have access to cash or sufficient reserves, a good credit rating, and a minimal number of canceled contracts. Diverse and sustainable funding is also important. Do funds come largely from fees for service or from grants? Does the contractor depend overly on one large client or source of funding?

Assessing organizational capacity involves examining the contractors' management and staffing capacity, internal performance analysis, and customer service orientation. Does the management team have expertise in education and a clear delineation of responsibilities? Is there sufficient staff? Does the staff have sufficient K-12 education experience? Is there a formal training program for new staff and ongoing professional development? Does the contractor conduct quality analyses of its work and solicit client feedback? Does it make changes based on what it learns? What kind of customer service resources are provided and are they readily available?

Hassel and Steiner (2004) also provide valuable recommendations and tools for selecting and dealing with contractors. They address such issues as putting together a selection team, writing a request for proposal, addressing common issues that arise during implementation, and establishing an evaluation plan.

8. Learn from others' experiences in replacing leaders and staff

Hassel et al. (2006) cite having the right leader as the most important factor in whether a turnaround will be successful. "The two major actions commonly taken by successful turnaround leaders include the following:

- Concentrating on a few very important changes with big, fast payoffs.
- Acting to implement practices proven to work with previously low-performing students even when they require deviations from district policies" (p. 81).

Other actions that contribute to success include:

- "Communicating a positive vision of future school results.
- Collecting and personally analyzing school and student performance data.
- Making an action plan based on data.
- Helping staff personally 'see and feel' the problems students face.
- Getting key influencers within district/school to support major changes.
- Measuring and reporting progress frequently and publicly.
- Gathering staff team often and requiring all involved in decision making to disclose and discuss their own results in open-air meetings.
- Funneling time and money into tactics that get results; halting unsuccessful tactics.
- Requiring all staff to change, not making this optional.
- Silencing change resisters indirectly by showing speedy successes.
- Acting in relentless pursuit of goals rather than touting progress as ultimate success" (p. 82).

Hassel et al. identify the following traits of successful turnaround leaders:

- Driving for results: setting high goals, taking initiative, being relentlessly persistent.
- Solving problems: using performance data to identify and solve immediate problems.
- Showing confidence: exhibiting confidence, using failure to initiate problem solving.
- Influence: influencing immediate action toward the school's goals.
- Teamwork and cooperation: getting input and keeping others informed.
- Conceptual thinking: connecting the mission, learning standards, and the curriculum.

- Team leadership: assuming the role as leader and motivating staff to perform.
- Organizational commitment: making personal sacrifices needed for school success.
- Communicating a compelling vision: rousing staff to commit energy to the change.

As with charter schools, principals need freedom to implement necessary changes, as well as ongoing support from the district (e.g., with student data, funding, communications), and help removing ineffective staff from the school. Similarly, establishing accountability for quick improvement and engaging stakeholders are critical as well.

Although a change in leadership generally precedes a successful turnaround, wholesale staff replacement is not usually needed. The essential thing is to have staff who support change. The capacity of existing staff to adapt to new responsibilities and goals is more important than any inherent benefits a clean slate might provide. Nonetheless, it may be necessary to remove some teachers who are unwilling to change.

9. Select improvement models with evidence of success

The What Works Clearinghouse, the Comprehensive School Reform Quality Center, the Center for Data-Driven Reform in Education, and the Northwest Regional Educational Laboratory are all sources of information on the efficacy of improvement models. In science, the accepted "gold standard" for evidence is a controlled experiment. Controlled experiments in education are rare and there are varying gradations of quality of evidence from the anecdotal to quasi-experiments. Some sources are more liberal than others in determining what research is rigorous enough to "count" (i.e., is reliable and credible). For that reason, not all sources will cite the same research.

As of this writing, the What Works Clearinghouse (www.whatworks.ed.gov) provides reports of rigorously screened research on programs in elementary and middle school mathematics, character education, dropout prevention, early childhood education, English language learning, and beginning reading.

The Northwest Regional Educational Laboratory maintains a catalog of school reform models at http://www.nwrel.org/scpd/catalog/index.shtml. It provides descriptive information for each model – grade levels, main features, whether subject-area programs are provided, special populations, materials, and parent involvement, among others – as well as a description of the general approach and research findings. There are explanations of the assistance provided by the developer and the costs associated with adoption. References to selected evaluation reports – those commissioned by the developer and those by independent researchers – are given along with demographic breakdowns and contact information (provided by the model developer) for schools using the program.

The Comprehensive School Reform Quality Center (CSRQ) has released reports on education service providers (2006), elementary school reform models (2005), middle and high school reform models (2006), and enhancing participation of students with disabilities in school reform models (n.d.). The models are rated on the extent to which there is evidence of:

- Positive effects on student achievement (overall, for diverse student populations, and in specific subject areas)
- Positive effects on additional student outcomes, such as attendance or dropout rates
- Positive effects on parent, family, and community involvement
- A link between research and the model's design
- Services and support to schools to enable successful implementation

Evidence was rated on how reliable and credible it was and whether the model's impact was large or small. Note that a low rating does not necessarily mean that a model is ineffective; a model may also have a low rating if it has not been the subject of sufficient rigorous research. The CSRQ reports also contain breakdowns of cost data by program year and detailed descriptions of the models and the services provided.

Other resources are also available. The Best Evidence Encyclopedia (http://www.bestevidence.org/) is a free web site created by the Johns Hopkins University Center for Data-Driven Reform in Education (CDDRE) that examines meta-analyses or other quantitative syntheses of educational research.

It is essential that you select a model that addresses your particular school's' needs; the model that worked at the school down the street might not be appropriate for your school if your needs differ from theirs. If your school's greatest need is to improve reading instruction, a model that emphasizes collaboration might not be the best choice, even though collaboration is a fine goal.

Selecting a reform model or educational service provider with a proven track record cannot guarantee success at your school, but it will clearly improve the odds. Keep in mind that implementation is key; even excellent models may falter if implementation is not faithful and complete.

10. Create optimum conditions for change

NWREL (2000), Hassel et al. (2006), Leverett (2004), Appelbaum (2002), and Redding (2006) all offer recommendations for how districts can create optimum conditions for successful restructuring. These include:

- Putting the right leader in each school

- Committing sufficient resources (time, money, staff, professional development, data support)
- Giving schools the freedom they need to make changes in instruction, organization, and scheduling even if those conflict with established district procedures
- Reorganizing district operations for a unified, coherent focus on support of instructional improvement, rather than compliance with district mandates
- Providing information on restructuring alternatives and assistance in dealing with contractors and holding them accountable
- Assigning each school a specially trained central office staff member who can serve as an effective liaison and resource to the school, rather than an enforcer or commanding officer
- Helping schools gather and use data
- Equitably allocating financial and staff resources
- Requiring accountability for both district and school staff and addressing failure promptly
- Creating a pipeline of turnaround leaders
- Facilitating professional networks and professional development tailored to each school's needs
- Providing schools with control over their own budgets
- Soliciting meaningful input from schools
- Building community support for change

NCEA's self-audit tool (http://www.just4kids.org/bestpractice/self_audit_framework.cfm?sub=tools) provides a means for districts to benchmark their practices to those of high-performing districts and gives some case studies. The story of Houston's use of aligned improvements vs. random improvements (http://www.just4kids.org/bestpractice/study_framework.cfm?sub=national& study=2003broad) and other Broad Prize winners and finalists illustrate how districts can foster change.

Conclusion

The path to successful restructuring begins with a careful look at a school's data and circumstances. An understanding of the change process – and possible pitfalls – can help the process run more smoothly.

There is no single best model for restructuring. Much depends on what resources are available and what models are most appropriate to each school's circumstances. Important considerations are quality leadership for each school, support from the district, input from the school, and a consideration of the evidence supporting the efficacy of possible interventions.

References

Academic Development Institute. (n.d.) *Managing change.* Lincoln, IL: Author.

Appelbaum, D. (2002). *The need for district support for school reform: What the researchers say.* Washington, DC: National Clearinghouse for Comprehensive School Reform. Retrieved Fall 2006 from http://www.csrclearinghouse.org/pubs/research/need02.pdf

Center for Comprehensive School Reform and Improvement. (n.d.). *Reallocating resources for school improvement – Guiding principles for allocating resources.* Retrieved Fall 2006 from http://www.centerforcsri.org/pubs/reallocation/principles.html

Center for Comprehensive School Reform and Improvement. (2006). *When the plan becomes part of the problem.* Retrieved Fall 2006 from http://www.centerforcsri.org/files/TheCenter_NL_Mar06.pdf

Center for Data-Driven Reform in Education. *Best evidence encyclopedia.* Retrieved Fall 2006 from http://www.bestevidence.org/

Center on Education Policy. (2006). *Wrestling the devil in the details: An early look at restructuring in California.* Washington, DC: Author. Retrieved Fall 2006 from http://www.cep-dc.org/improvingpublicschools/WrestlingDetails.pdf

Center on Innovation and Improvement. (n.d.). (Reports by state or regional center). Retrieved Fall 2006 from http://www.centerii.org/centerIIPublic/criteria.aspx

Comprehensive School Reform Quality Center. (2005). *CSRQ report on elementary comprehensive school reform models.* Washington, DC: Author. Retrieved Fall 2006 from http://www.csrq.org/CSRQreportselementaryschoolreport.asp

Comprehensive School Reform Quality Center. (2006). *CSRQ report on middle and high school comprehensive school reform models.* Washington, DC: Author. Retrieved Fall 2006 from http://www.csrq.org/documents/MSHS2006Report_FinalFullVersion10-03-06.pdf

Comprehensive School Reform Quality Center. (2006). *CSRQ report on education service providers.* Washington, DC: Author. Retrieved Fall 2006 from http://www.csrq.org/espreport.asp

Comprehensive School Reform Quality Center and The Finance Project. (2006). *Choosing an education contractor: A guide to assessing financial and organizational capacity.* Washington, DC: Authors. Retrieved Fall 2006 from http://www.financeproject.org/publications/CSRQConsumerGuide.pdf

Comprehensive School Reform Quality Center. (n.d.) *Enhancing the participation of students with disabilities in comprehensive school reform models.* Retrieved Fall 2006 from http://www.csrq.org/documents/EnhancingtheParticipationofStudentswithDisabilitiesinCSRModels.pdf

Fox, D. (2005). *Look before you leap: Responding effectively to Year 4 requirements, A guide for selecting alternative forms of governance and restructuring for PI Year 4 schools.* Los Angeles: Southern California Comprehensive Assistance Center. Retrieved Fall 2006 from http://www.sccoe.org/depts/sas/docs/look_before_you_leap.pdf

Hassel, E. A., Hassel, B. C., Arkin, M. D., Kowal, J. M., & Steiner, L. M. (2006). *School restructuring under No Child Left Behind: What works when? A guide for education leaders.* Washington, DC: Learning Point Associates. Retrieved Fall 2006 from http://www.centerforcsri.org/files/RestructuringGuide.pdf

Hassel, B., & Steiner, L. (2004). *Guide to working with external providers.* Oak Brook, IL: North Central Regional Educational Laboratory. Retrieved Fall 2006 from http://www.centerforcsri.org/pubs/ExternalProviders.pdf

Leverett, L. (2004). *Beyond the emperor's new clothes: The role of the central office in systemwide instructional improvement.* Washington, DC: National Clearinghouse for Comprehensive School Reform. Retrieved Fall 2006 from http://www.centerforcsri.org/pubs/bench/benchsum04.pdf

Mid-continent Research for Education and Learning. (2003). *Sustaining school improvement: Resource allocation.* Retrieved Fall 2006 from http://www.mcrel.org/PDF/LeadershipOrganizationDevelopment/5031TG_resourcefolio.pdf

National Center for Educational Accountability. *Self-audits.* Retrieved Fall 2006 from http://www.just4kids.org/bestpractice/self_audit_framework.cfm?sub=tools

No Child Left Behind Act, Sec. 1116, 20 U.S.C.A. § 6301-6578. (2002) (enacted).

Northwest Regional Educational Laboratory. (2005, last updated 10/4/06). *Catalog of school reform models.* Retrieved Fall 2006 from http://www.nwrel.org/scpd/catalog/index.shtml

Redding, S. (2006). *The Mega System: Deciding. Learning. Connecting.* Lincoln, IL: Academic Development Institute.

Reinventing Education. (n.d.). *Change toolkit.* Retrieved Fall 2006 from http://www.reinventingeducation.org/RE3Web/

Schmoker, M. (2004, February). Tipping point: From feckless reform to substantive instructional improvement. *Phi Delta Kappan, 85*(6), 424-432. Retrieved Fall 2006 from http://pdkintl.org/kappan/k0402sch.htm

U.S. Department of Education. (2006). *LEA and school improvement: Non-regulatory guidance.* Washington, DC: Author.

About the Author

Carole L. Perlman, before joining the Center on Innovation and Improvement as a Technical Advisor, served as School Improvement Coordinator for the Chicago Public Schools from 2003 to 2006. For 20 years she was director of student assessment for the Chicago Public Schools. She holds a B.S. in Mathematics with honors from the University of Illinois at Chicago (UIC), an M.S. in Statistics from the University if Illinois at Urbana-Champaign and a doctorate in Public Policy Analysis from UIC. A past president of the National Association of Test Directors (NATD) and past board member of the National Council on Measurement in Education (NCME), she also served on the Center for Research on Evaluation, Standards, and Student Testing (CRESST) National Advisory Board and represented NCME for two terms on the Joint Committee on Testing Practices. She has served on numerous state and federal advisory panels, including the 1992 NAEP Reading Framework Steering Committee, the first NAEP Mathematics Standard-Setting Panel, the Education Information Advisory Committee's Assessment Task Force, and the Voluntary National Test Technical Advisory Committee. She is a frequent presenter at professional conferences and is the recipient of the AERA Division D Research Report Award, National Association of Test Directors Career Award for Outstanding Contributions to Educational Assessment, and the UIC College of Education's Distinguished Alumna Award.

4. Restructuring Through Learning-Focused Leadership

Joseph Murphy

This review provides a portrait of learning-focused leadership.

Abstract

Over the last three decades, we have learned that leadership is a key element in the school and district improvement algorithm. We have also discovered that a particular type of leadership – learning-focused leadership – character-izes high-performing schools and school districts. Of particular importance here, we are also learning that these truths about leadership are especially rele-vant in turning around failing schools in general and "restructuring schools" in particular. In this analysis of the effective schools and school improvement lit-erature from 1975-2005, we isolate ten principles of leadership that define the learning-focused leadership that is linked to helping troubled schools recover.

Introduction

Over the last half century a great deal has been written about the impor-tance of leadership in general and in relation to organizational performance in particular. Academics, practitioners, and reviewers from every field of study have concluded that leadership is a central variable in the equation that defines organizational success (Bennis & Nanus, 1985). In particular, they consistently highlight leadership as the cardinal element in turning around failing organi-zations (Murphy & Meyers, in press). Looking specifically at education, we

Handbook on Restructuring and Substantial School Improvement
Copyright © 2007 by Information Age Publishing and The Academic Development Institute
63

have parallel evidence that leadership is a central ingredient – and often the keystone element – in school and district success as defined in terms of student achievement (Leithwood, Louis, Anderson, & Wahlstrom, 2004; Marzano, Waters, & McNulty, 2005; Murphy & Hallinger, 1988). And as is the case with other organizations, leadership is a hallmark ingredient in the recovery of failing schools (e.g., restructuring schools under NCLB).

An assortment of researchers over the last three decades has helped us see that not all leadership is equal, that a particular type of leadership is especially visible in high-performing schools and school districts. This strand can best be labeled "leadership for learning," "instructionally focused leadership," or "leadership for school improvement" (see Murphy, 1990 and Beck & Murphy, 1996 for reviews), or learning-focused leadership. The touchstones for this strand of leadership include the ability of leaders (a) to stay consistently focused on the right stuff – the core technology of schooling, or learning, teaching, curriculum, and assessment, and (b) to make all the other dimensions of schooling (e.g., administration, organization, finance) work in the service of a more robust core technology and improved student learning.

In this paper, we examine the components of learning-focused leadership employing research on effective schools and school districts and high-performing principals and superintendents that can be linked to the reintegration of troubled schools under the restructuring platform provided by NCLB. We capture the knowledge base under ten key principles.

Principles

1. Develop and steward vision

Leaders in high-performing schools devote considerable energy to "the development, articulation, implementation, and stewardship of a vision of learning that is shared and supported by the school community" (Council of Chief State School Officers, 1996, p. 10). On the development end of the continuum, leaders ensure that the vision and mission of the school are crafted with and among stakeholders. They also ensure that a variety of sources of data that illuminate student learning are used in the forging of vision and goals. In particular, they make certain that (a) assessment data related to student learning, (b) demographic data pertaining to students and the community, and (c) information on patterns of opportunity to learn are featured in the development process.

Effective leaders facilitate the creation of a school vision that reflects high and appropriate standards of learning, a belief in the educability of all students, and high levels of personal and organizational performance. They emphasize ambitious goals, ones that call for improvement over the status quo. In particular, leadership for school improvement means making certain that goals are focused on students, feature student learning and achievement, and are clearly defined. Learning-focused leaders ensure that responsibility for achieving targets are made explicit and that timelines for achieving objectives are specified. In short, they make sure that the school vision is translated into specific and measurable end results. They also ensure that the resources needed to meet goals are clearly identified – and made available to the school community.

Effective principals and other school-based leaders articulate the vision through personal modeling and by communicating with others in and around the organization. On the first front, they are adept at making the school vision central to their own daily work. They demonstrate through their actions the organization's commitment to the values and beliefs at the heart of the mission as well as to the specific activities needed to reach goals. On the second issue, communication, learning-focused leaders work ceaselessly to promote the school's mission and agenda to staff, students, parents, and members of the extended school community (e.g., business and religious leaders, district office staff). Indeed, effective leaders are masters in keeping vision, mission, and goals in the forefront of everyone's attention and at the center of everyone's work. To accomplish this, they engage a wide array of formal and informal avenues of exchange and employ a variety of techniques (e.g., symbols, ceremonies).

Master leaders are especially well versed at translating vision into operation and at stewarding the school's vision. They are careful monitors, (a) ensuring a continuous examination of assumptions, beliefs, and values, (b) assessing implementation of goals, and (c) evaluating the impact of school objectives on organizational performance and student learning. One way these leaders shepherd goals is through the actions they take to recognize, celebrate, and reward the contributions of community members to the development, the implementation, and, most importantly, the realization of school goals. At the same time, they do not overlook shortcomings and failures. Certainly a critical dimension of operationalizing and stewarding is seeing to it that school vision and school goals shape routine school activities and anchor organizational systems and structures. On a personal front, operationalizing and shepherding occurs when leaders act as keepers and promoters of the vision; maintain enthusiasm and a sense of optimism, especially in periods of waning energy; and inspire others to break through barriers to make the school vision a reality.

2. Hire, allocate, and support quality staff

As NCLB helps us see, teachers are the keystone of quality education in schools where all youngsters reach ambitious learning targets. Therefore, effective leaders devote considerable time and undertake much careful planning to guarantee that the school is populated with excellent teachers, and with colleagues whose values and instructional frameworks are consistent with the mission and the culture of the school. Indeed, such action is at the heart of the restructuring options provided by NCLB (see Hassel et al., introduction to this volume). Learning-focused leaders are also diligent in assigning teachers to various responsibilities. They allocate teachers based on educational criteria, especially student needs, rather than on less appropriate foundations such as staff seniority and school politics.

Learning-focused leaders devote abundant time to supporting colleagues in their efforts to strengthen teaching and learning in and across classrooms. Foremost, they are aggressive in identifying and removing barriers that prevent colleagues from doing their work well. They provide intellectual stimulation and make certain that teachers have a high quality stream of job-embedded opportunities to expand, enhance, and refine their repertoires of instructional skills. They also make sure that the materials that teachers require to perform their jobs are on hand in sufficient quantity and in a timely fashion. Consistent with the involvement and investment theme, effective leaders demonstrate personal interest in staff and make themselves available to them.

We know from the literature that feedback about performance is essential to the learning process, and leaders in high-performing schools are diligent about providing this information to colleagues on a consistent basis and in a timely manner. In supplying performance feedback, learning-focused leaders (a) rely on personal knowledge developed through numerous classroom observations, both informal and formal, and (b) employ a variety of supervisory and evaluation strategies. They make student learning the calculus of the exchange process. Effective leaders are especially expert in opening up a wide assortment of improvement opportunities for teachers. And they are relentless in counseling poor teachers to leave the profession. In a related vein, improvement-focused leaders aggressively monitor the instructional program in its entirety, assuring alignment between learning standards and objectives and classroom instruction.

Implicit in the NCLB restructuring options is the understanding that academic learning time is the caldron in which student achievement materializes. And we know that effective leaders work tirelessly with staff to ensure that this precious resource is maximized. They begin by making sure that the great bulk of time is devoted to instructional activities, that non-instructional time is kept to a minimum. They also see to it that the majority of instructional time is dedicated to core academic subjects. Within this learning space, they work with teachers to accentuate the use of instructional strategies that maximize student engagement at high levels of success. On a parallel track, learning-focused leaders undertake an array of activities that protect valuable instructional time from interruptions, including (a) assigning academic subjects time slots that are least likely to be disturbed by school events; (b) protecting teachers from distractions from the school office; (c) developing, implementing, and monitoring procedures to reduce student tardiness and absenteeism; and (d) ensuring that teachers are punctual. They also foster more productive use of time by coordinating time usage among teachers and across classes (e.g., all language arts instruction unfolding during the first two hours of the day).

3. Maximize content coverage in an aligned curriculum

There is considerable evidence that content coverage is perhaps the most important variable in explaining student academic achievement. Not surprisingly, therefore, we know that the men and women who lead schools where all youngsters reach high targets of performance are attentive to this critical function. They work with colleagues to ensure that the school is defined by a rigorous curricular program in general and that each student's program in particular is of high quality. On the first issue, they establish high standards and expectations in the various curricular domains consistent with blueprints crafted by professional associations and learned societies. On the second topic, they ensure that opportunity to learn is maximized for each youngster. These leaders are also diligent in monitoring and evaluating the effectiveness of the school's curricular program.

In the array of factors that define high-performing schools, curriculum alignment enjoys a position of exceptional prominence, and effective leaders are especially attentive to creating a "tightly coupled curriculum" (Murphy, Weil, Hallinger, & Mitman, 1985, p. 367) throughout the school. This means that they ensure that objectives (standards), instruction, curriculum materials, and assessments are all carefully coordinated. It also means that all special programs (e.g., bilingual education) are brought into the gravitational field of the regular program. Finally, it means that there is a high degree of coordination (a) across subjects within grades, (b) across grade levels and phases of schooling (e.g., from the elementary to the middle school), and (c) among teachers within and across departments and grade levels.

4. Monitor student progress

NCLB tells us that rigorous monitoring of student learning fuels restructuring efforts, both in terms of the call to action and the hammer of accountability. Learning-focused leaders, therefore, actively monitor student progress. They promote a serious attitude toward test taking among staff and students.

Instructionally effective schools emphasize both standardized and criterion-referenced testing. Tests are used to diagnose programmatic and student strengths and weaknesses, to evaluate the results of changes in the school's instructional program, and to make classroom assignments. In particular, they are used to judge the effectiveness of school restructuring efforts undertaken in response to NCLB. Researchers have discovered that the principals who lead these schools practice a wide variety of monitoring behaviors: They encourage the establishment and use of testing programs; they provide teachers with test results in a timely and useful fashion; they discuss test results with the staff as a whole and with grade-level and specialty-area staff and individual teachers; they provide interpretive analyses that describe the test data in a concise form for teachers; and they underscore the use of test results for setting goals, assessing the curriculum, evaluating instruction, and measuring progress toward school goals. Learning-focused leaders also ensure that student progress is regularly and precisely reported to parents.

5. Establish positive expectations for academic learning

School learning climate refers to the "norms, beliefs and attitudes reflected in instructional patterns and behavioral practices that enhance or impede student achievement" (Lezotte, Hathaway, Miller, Passalacqua, & Brookover, 1980, p. 4). Studies of schooling show that teaching performance and student outcomes are as much a function of this ethos or environment as they are of the personal qualities and abilities of teachers. They also demonstrate that for both teachers and parents the principal is a central element in the school climate equation. And this finding is even more salient in schools on the road to recovery under NCLB.

The principal's functions here deal with those elements of the school learning climate that are most directly related to the teaching-learning process in classrooms. These functions are heavily task-oriented. The functions in the supportive work environment, on the other hand, have more of a maintenance orientation, affect learning tasks only indirectly, and often require the principal to operate in a boundary spanning role with the larger school environment. Principals foster the development of a school learning climate conducive to teaching and learning by establishing positive expectations and standards, maintaining high visibility, providing incentives for teachers and students, and promoting professional development.

Studies in classrooms in schools that fail to meet AYP have shown that teachers often hold inappropriately low expectations for low ability students and for low ability instructional and curricular groups. These reduced expectations, in turn, are often translated into teacher behaviors that disadvantage these students in terms of academic performance. Studies of administrators at schools with particularly high and low levels of student achievement affirm these conclusions at the school level as well – inappropriately low expectations are often held for schools with high concentrations of minority and poor students and for low ability tracks within schools.

In contrast to these findings, researchers have discovered that principals in schools with high levels of student achievement are actively involved in defining high academic and behavioral expectations for their students and are less likely to base expectations on adult beliefs about the biosocial characteristics of students. Research shows that learning-focused leaders translate this attitude into school policies and practices that reflect and define positive expectations for students in the following ways: They place more instructional demands on teachers; they communicate their concern for and interest in student achievement; they establish clearly defined schoolwide academic standards; they develop standards that apply to *all* students; they hold more specific expectations than their less effective peers; they create policies that encourage students to pursue more rigorous academic goals; they hold adults responsible for learning outcomes; they couple success with performance; and they require student mastery of grade level skills prior to entry in the following grade.

6. Maintain high visibility and involvement

Visibility refers to the presence of the principal on the school campus and in classrooms. High visibility by executives has been called management by touring around. In schools, this touring has been associated with positive effects on students' and teachers' attitudes and behaviors. Although the evidence is not conclusive, researchers generally find that learning-focused leaders spend more time in classrooms and on the school campus than does the average school administrator.

Personal involvement means that these administrators are directly involved in leading the school's educational program. Leaders in turnaround organizations in general and highly productive schools in particular have a strong orientation to and affinity for the core technology of their business – learning and teaching in the education enterprise. In the area of pedagogy, they are knowledgeable about and deeply involved in the instructional program of the school and are heavily invested in instruction, spending considerable time on the teaching function. They model the importance of teaching by being directly involved in the design and implementation of the instructional program. They are also knowledgeable about and heavily invested in the curricular program of the school. Finally, they are knowledgeable about assessment practices and personally involved with colleagues in crafting, implementing, and monitoring assessment systems at the classroom and school levels and in checking the effectiveness of NCLB school restructuring work.

7. Promote student and teacher incentives

Another aspect of the learning-focused leadership role in creating a positive learning climate involves setting up a work structure that rewards and recognizes teachers for their efforts. Principals have few discretionary rewards to use with teachers. The single salary schedule and the tenure system severely limit principals' ability to motivate teachers. However, research has begun to show that money is not the only way to reward high levels of performance. Specifically, principals can provide recognition to teachers by distributing leadership, showing personal interest, providing public acknowledgment before colleagues and parents, and giving private praise and encouragement.

There is also evidence that learning-focused leaders use rewards and recognition of students to help establish a school learning climate where academic achievement is valued. Effective leaders institute schoolwide recognition systems. They are the key actors in linking classroom and school reward systems, ensuring that they are mutually supportive. They are also actively involved in providing personal recognition to individual students. Principals in effective schools make sure that rewards are given frequently and that they reach a high percentage of students. Although rewards are distributed for a variety of reasons, in schools led by effective administrators, special emphasis is given to recognizing academic excellence. Finally, effective principals often establish student reward programs that are both public in nature and closely connected in time to the behavior for which recognition is given.

8. Promote professional development and practice

A number of researchers find that principal support for and involvement in teacher professional development activities characterize effective schools, findings that parallel the human capacity-building work of leaders in turnaround organizations in the corporate and government sectors generally and in restructuring schools in particular. Administrator attention and support has also been linked to more effective implementation of professional development activities and institutionalization of improvement efforts generally. Principals in effective schools are committed to helping teachers improve their skills and teaching strategies. They focus staff development activities on the entire staff and on the specific goals and curriculum programs of the school. They are especially adept at using informal coalitions of teachers in implementing new programs. They take an active role in planning, participating in, and evaluating professional development activities with their staffs. Research also reveals that learning-focused leaders provide both direct aid (e.g., concrete technical assistance and materials) and indirect support (e.g., encouragement) to teachers as they attempt to integrate skills learned during staff development programs into their repertoire of instructional behaviors. Effective principals facilitate opportunities for professional growth by enabling teachers to attend conferences, establishing mechanisms that facilitate the exchange of professional dialogue, and personally sharing ideas and materials with staff.

Leaders of schools on the crest of the improvement curve actively promote the formation of a learning organization, the development of staff cohesion and support, and the growth of communities of professional practice. At the broadest level, these leaders endeavor to create a culture of collaboration and the systems, operations, and policies that provide the infrastructure for that collegial culture. At this level, they also are active in building shared beliefs about the importance of community. They nurture collaborative processes (e.g., shared decision making), forge schedules (e.g., common planning time), and create organizational structures (e.g., team leadership) that permit and encourage shared mission and direction, collaborative work, and mutual accountability for school goals and student learning. These leaders are particularly attentive to ensuring that there are a variety of mechanisms for teachers to communicate and work among themselves. And, to be sure, these women and men are active participants in the various school learning communities, often serving key linking and pollinating roles in the process. They understand, and help others understand, that communities of professional practice offer the most appropriate vessels for professional learning and the forging of new instructional skills. Finally, they take advantage of the fact that they are in a unique position to garner and allocate resources to bring communities of professional practice to life.

9. Develop a supportive work environment

Studies of school effects and program improvement have shown that especially effective schools establish important organizational structures and processes that support the teaching-learning process. In these organizations, administrators are actively engaged in creating safe and orderly learning environments, providing opportunities for meaningful student involvement, developing collaboration and cohesion among staff, securing outside support for school goals, and forging links between the school and the larger community. As we noted earlier, the functions in this area of the framework are less directly connected to the teaching-learning process occurring in classrooms, that is, they are less directly task-oriented. In addition, they often require the principal to work with actors (e.g., parents, business leaders) in the larger school environment.

Effective schools are characterized by learning environments that are safe and orderly without being oppressive and by physical environments that are clean and well maintained. It is also clear that the development of the learning environments in these schools is due in large part to the leadership of the principal. Learning-focused leaders seem to be more concerned than their colleagues with the management and discipline tone of their schools. They work with individual teachers to insure the use of effective classroom management practices. More importantly, they create consistency and coordination in the school discipline program. This last point is of particular consequence because studies of effective schools find that "the particular rules and approaches to discipline may be less important than the existence of some generally recognized and accepted set of standards" (Rutter et al., 1979, p. 121).

Studies show that effective principals work with their staffs to ensure that: (a) school rules and consequences are clearly defined, communicated, and understood by students, teachers, and parents; (b) rules are fairly and consistently enforced; and (c) classroom and school rules are integrally connected. They (a) model appropriate behavior by personally enforcing discipline with students; (b) often involve teachers and students in the development of school rules; (c) secure support for school rules; (d) see that all staff members support and enforce discipline procedures; (e) confront problems quickly and forcefully; (f) provide support for the management system (e.g., student detention and recognition programs); and (g) support teachers with discipline problems in their classrooms.

Successful schools are adept at bonding students to important adult academic and social values and norms. This bonding helps prevent the development of student cultures that are often inimical to the preferred outcomes of the school. Learning-focused leaders operate in these schools to promote meaningful opportunities for student involvement by establishing system-wide activity programs, encouraging teachers and students to become involved in these activities, providing rewards and recognition for successful student participation, and promoting the widespread use of school symbols (e.g., school jackets and t-shirts) that both distinguish the school from the larger community and clearly mark students as members of the school.

The opportunity for students to be meaningfully involved in school activities has been noted in some effective school studies. This finding receives support from studies of the effects of extracurricular activities on student learning and from independent work in the area of juvenile delinquency prevention. The components of this factor are opportunities for students to (a) learn responsibility and practice leadership behavior; (b) form ties to the school and to appropriate adult role models; and (c) develop the skills necessary to participate successfully in activities.

Collaborative organizational processes that bring staff together to plan, make decisions, and resolve conflicts about instruction and curriculum are often found in effective schools and successful improvement programs. While principals in effective schools promote staff collaboration, teachers working with less effective instructional leaders function more as individuals than as members of a school team – "in the less successful schools, teachers were often left completely alone to plan what to teach, with little guidance from their senior colleagues and little coordination with other teachers" (Rutter et al., 1979, p. 136). Collaborative activities that do occur in these less successful schools are more socially based and less professionally oriented than the exchanges that occur in schools with more effective instructional leaders.

Research shows that learning-focused leaders employ the following structural activities to facilitate the development of staff collaboration: developing schoolwide goals and objectives and clearly articulating the rationale and foci of new programs; establishing and using formal mechanisms for professional interchanges (e.g., staff meetings, professional development activities, common planning periods); promoting staff stability; providing resources and a supportive work milieu for cooperative planning; giving faculty a formal role in communication and decision making; and using a variety of methods of decision making. On a less formal level, learning-focused leaders promote staff collaboration by discussing instructional issues regularly in informal exchanges with teachers, by soliciting teachers' opinions, by showing respect and consideration for staff and their ideas, and by encouraging direct, informal communication among staff.

More effective schools often have administrators that are skilled in obtaining supplemental resources for teachers and students. To begin with, these schools are more adept in attracting additional funds and materials from the community. Learning-focused leaders are also often more powerful in their districts. They use the formal and informal channels at their disposal to influence district-level decision making and to better the competitive position of their schools in the distribution of power and resources. Effective principals seem to be more active than their peers in obtaining resources – an outcome consistent with the findings of the general body of research on educational organizations. For example, while their less effective colleagues often follow standard procedures in hiring and transferring staff, effective principals take assertive action to shape their staffs according to the philosophy and objectives of the school. Finally, learning-focused leaders allocate money and other resources based on school goals. This goal-directed administrative behavior is often conspicuous by its absence in less effective schools.

10. Forge home-school links

In many schools that fail to reach AYP, there is a profound disconnect between the school and it customers – parents and members of the larger community. Indeed, the legitimization of customer voice is deeply woven into NCLB restructuring options. Many highly successful schools, in turn, have high levels of parental involvement and support. Although almost all forms of parental involvement and support have been shown to have some positive effects on student achievement, the most effective type is that which focuses attention on the primary mission of educating students, that is, in which parents support at school and at home the academic activities that are occurring in the classroom. In addition to improved academic performance, parent interest has been linked to increased political support and maintenance of legitimacy in the larger environment surrounding the school. Specific activities in the area of home-school relations that have been attributed to instructional leaders include: communicating with parents on a regular basis, including informing parents of programs and activities; obtaining human resources for both regular and extracurricular programs; establishing programs that promote contact between teachers and parents; interacting personally to promote the school to important community groups; providing educational activities and other programs for parents to learn about the curriculum used to teach their children; and developing systems that parents can use to work with their children at home on the academic skills being stressed in the school program.

Conclusion

In this review we spotlight the type of leadership – learning-focused leadership – that is central to the task of improving schools in general and restructuring schools under NCLB in particular. We undertook that assignment by examining the literature on effective schools and school improvement. The framework that emerged is comprised of 10 principle-based functions.

References

Beck, L. G., & Murphy, J. (1996). *The four imperatives of a successful school.* Thousand Oaks, CA: Corwin.

Bennis, W., & Nanus, B. (1985). *Leaders: The strategies for taking charge.* New York: Harper & Row.

Council of Chief State School Officers (1996). *Interstate school leaders licensure consortium: Standards for school leaders.* Washington, DC: Author.

Leithwood, K., Louis, K. S., Anderson, S., & Wahlstrom, K. (2004). *How leadership influences student learning* (paper commissioned by the Wallace Foundation). Minneapolis: University of Minnesota.

Lezotte, L., Hathaway, D. V., Miller, S. K., Passalacqua, J., & Brookover, W. B. (1980). *School learning climate and student achievement: A social system approach to increased student learning*. Tallahassee: The Site Specific Technical Assistance Center, Florida State University Foundation.

Marzano, R. J., Waters, T., & McNulty, B. A. (2005). *School leadership that works: From research to results*. Alexandria, VA: Association for Supervision and Curriculum Development.

Murphy, J. (1990). Principal instructional leadership. In L. L. Lotto & P. W. Thurston (Eds.), *Advances in educational administration: Changing perspectives on the school*. (Vol. I, Part B, pp. 163-200). Greenwich, CT: JAI Press.

Murphy, J., & Hallinger, P. (1988, February). The characteristics of instructionally effective school districts. *Journal of Educational Research, 81*(3), 176-181.

Murphy, J., & Meyers, C. V. (in press). *Turning around failing schools: Lessons from the organizational sciences*. Thousand Oaks, CA: Corwin.

Murphy J., Weil, M., Hallinger, P., & Mitman, A. (1985, Spring). School effectiveness: A conceptual framework. *The Educational Forum, 49*(3), 361-374.

Rutter, M., Maughan, B., Mortimore, P., & Ouston, J. (1979). *Fifteen thousand hours: Secondary schools and their effects on children*. Cambridge, MA: Harvard University Press.

About the Author

Joseph Murphy is Associate Dean and Professor of Education at Peabody College of Education of Vanderbilt University and a member of the Center on Innovation & Improvement's Scientific Council. In the public schools, he has served as an administrator at the school, district, and state levels, including an appointment as the Executive Assistant to the Chief Deputy Superintendent of Public Instruction in California. His most recent appointment was as the founding President of the Ohio Principals Leadership Academy. He was the founding Chair (1994-2004) of the Interstate School Leaders Licensure Consortium (ISLLC) and directed the development of the *ISLLC Standards for School Leaders*. Murphy is the co-editor of the *AERA Handbook of Research on Education Administration* (1999) and editor of the National Society for the Study of Education (NSSE) yearbook *The Educational Leadership Challenge* (2002). His work is in the area of school improvement, with special emphasis on leadership and policy. He has authored or co-authored 14 books and 2 major monographs in this area and edited another 11 books. His most recently authored volumes include: *Understanding and Assessing the Charter School Movement* (2002), *Leadership for Literacy* (2004), *Connecting Teacher Leadership and School Improvement* (2005), and *Preparing School Leaders: An Agenda for Research and Action* (2006).

5. Changing and Monitoring Instruction

Herbert J. Walberg

To improve achievement, focus instruction and assessment on state standards, employ assessment to evaluate students' progress, and employ instruction selectively to bring all students to proficiency.

Abstract

Improvement in achievement takes place most directly at the classroom level. For substantial improvement in achievement, the focus should be at this level and emphasize effective instruction and assessment aligned with state educational standards. Formative assessment should be continuing to determine the extent to which instruction is effective. Summative testing should be employed to determine the extent that students have attained proficiency. Frequent testing allows teachers to monitor each student's progress to determine the need for re-teaching and extending learning time. Test results and monitoring of classroom teaching practices are useful in determining what best helps students attain proficiency. If tests and classroom observations indicate that a particular method of teaching appears ineffective, another method should be chosen. Since students spend only about eight percent of the hours in the first 18 years of life in school, parents can be recruited to enrich the academic stimulation that takes place at home and in the community.

Introduction

This module concentrates on how classroom teaching and assessment can best be improved and draws upon syntheses of many studies of teaching. Be-

Handbook on Restructuring and Substantial School Improvement

Copyright © 2007 by Information Age Publishing and The Academic Development Institute

ginning in the early 1960s, researchers began systematic investigations of the effectiveness of teaching methods in promoting students' achievement. In what was called "process-product research," they measured the gains made by the teachers who had used particular methods of teaching such as direct instruction or conditions such as class size to determine whether these were associated with greater learning.

The bulk of these studies were "quasi-experiments" in which student progress from a pre-test to a post-test of the material to be learned was measured. With time, however, more and more studies employed randomization in true experiments in which students or classrooms were assigned to alternative methods or conditions randomly, as in a coin flip. As in medical fields, experiments are often considered the "gold standard" of scientific rigor.

The studies accumulated and became too voluminous for educators and even researchers to digest. For this reason, investigators began statistically analyzing the results of studies of particular methods of teaching and classroom conditions such as class size. These "meta-analyses" usually constitute a better scientific foundation than any single study that may be flawed in some unknown way. Other things being equal, moreover, methods and conditions that have not only strong but consistent effects are most useful since multiple studies are likely to have been carried out in different places, grade levels, and kinds of students and their communities. For these reasons, this module draws heavily on syntheses of many studies.

Some readers may wish to review the underlying basis for the principles in this module and see further discussion and illustrations of them. They may find the references at the end helpful. Specifically, Subotnik and Walberg's (2006) edited collection *The Scientific Basis of Educational Productivity* explains how experiments, quasi-experiments, and other research methods can put the practice of education on a firmer scientific base; this work also has a summary of many research syntheses.

Cawelti's (2004) *Handbook of Research on Improving Student Achievement* has chapters by national experts on high-performing school systems, effective general practices, staff development, and on teaching in the arts, foreign languages, health education, language arts, oral communications, mathematics, physical education, science, and social studies. Because of No Child Left Behind requirements, the chapters on language arts, mathematics, and science should be particularly useful in restructuring schools. For general principles of teaching, see Marzano, Pickering, and Pollock's (2001) *Classroom Instruction That Works: Research-Based Strategies for Increasing Student Achievement*.

A series of pamphlets by world experts commissioned by the International Academy of Education and published by the United Nations Educational, Scientific, and Cultural Organization ("UNESCO") are available without charge for download, instant printing of single copies, and re-publication of multiple copies. One of the booklets, *Using New Media* by Shih and Weekly (2006), explains how the booklets and other Internet media can be downloaded and distributed in hard copy, CDs, and DVDs. Those particularly useful for re-structuring schools are by Brophy (1999) on teaching; Redding (2000) on encouraging effective parental practices; Pang, Muaka, Bernhardt, and Kamil (2003) on reading; Topping (2000) on tutoring; and Wallace, Stariha, and Walberg (2004) on language arts. Because of the centrality of reading for much of learning, the more extended work *Successful Reading Instruction* edited by Kamil and colleagues may be usefully consulted.

No Child Left Behind requires progress by major racial-ethnic groups. Two edited works by national experts on this subject are Taylor's (2006) *Addressing The Achievement Gap: Findings And Applications* and Paik and Walberg's (2007) *Narrowing The Achievement Gap: Strategies For Educating Latino, Black, And Asian Students*.

Finally, classroom teaching takes place in the larger contexts of the school and community. For an analysis of these settings, see Redding's (2006) *The Mega System: Deciding. Learning. Connecting: A Handbook for Continuous Improvement Within a Community of the School*. This book shows how instruction and assessment can best be coordinated with leadership, research, curriculum, and professional development. Another broad work, *Best Practices of High-Performing School Systems* (Just for Kids, n.d.), is available on the Internet. It examines: curriculum and academic goals; staff selection, leadership, and capacity building; instructional programs, practices, and arrangements; and monitoring. It shows how these can be enacted systematically and simultaneously in the district, school, and classroom and gives many examples of how school districts implemented apparently successful programs.

Principles

1. Align instruction with state standards

In considering state standards, it is useful to remember that the No Child Left Behind federal legislation requires annual tests for all students in reading and mathematics in grades 3-8 and once in high school. With the goal of proficiency by 2013-2014, the data must be disaggregated for subgroups, and parents must be clearly informed about the quality of their child's school. Schools failing to make "Adequate Yearly Progress" (AYP) for the various subgroups face escalating sanctions, such as having to inform parents that their child is in a failing school, being required to allow their students to transfer to successful schools, replacing the staff, and, if failure continues, possible closure. Thus, particularly in the later stages, restructuring is a very serious matter.

How can progress be made? Since progress in proficiency is measured on state assessments of their own standards, they are the logical and most constructive starting point for planning improvements. District and school staff can make a careful analysis of their state standards for each grade level (Chubb, 2005; Just for Kids, 2006; Redding, 2006). One useful approach is for district authorities and those assigned to each grade to take responsibility for a given grade or combination of grades. They can first set forth knowledge, skill, and other standards requirements for that grade. They can then examine the degree to which the standards are covered in any special district and school requirements, in textbooks and other instructional materials, and in lesson plans of individual teachers or groups.

It is then helpful for staff to examine whether some of the standards requirements are taught in previous grades. If so, they can avoid unnecessary duplication or simply plan to provide some initial review and assessment of what students should know. Staff can also review the prerequisites to the requirements to be sure they are provided in previous grade levels. To ensure grade level continuity, staff with responsibilities for a given grade can meet with those of adjacent grade levels.

2. Align computer-managed summative testing with state standards

In the present discussion of restructuring schools, summative testing or assessment means the estimation of the degree that NCLB-required state standards are being met or are likely to be met. Ideally, the likelihood of making AYP could be measured continuously. But that ideal cannot as yet be attained.

Computer-administered tests, however, offer the prospect of periodic assessments during the school year (Chubb, 2005). For example, a consortium of school districts, the not-for-profit Northwest Evaluation Association (NWEA), has made impressive advances toward the end of reliable and high-quality assessments administered several times during the academic year and are now being used in approximately 6,000 schools around the country. Computer administered and managed, such tests have several other impressive advantages. They can, for example, be correlated with state achievement standards, and an estimate can be made of the likelihood of making AYP. Some states are considering the adoption of such tests rather than engaging in difficult and costly development of their own unique examinations. An early adopter of computer-managed tests, the Hot Springs, Arkansas school district, remains highly pleased with the tests.

Students' scores are available immediately as they complete the test, and overall school and detailed reports are returned within 24 hours after the last student finishes the test. The scores can be broken out by NCLB categories. Such tests can be "vertically scaled," that is, they yield scores comparable across grades. They are particularly desirable for measuring value-added and adequate yearly student progress. Like a yardstick capable of measuring both long and short objects, vertically scaled tests can compare the progress of students, classes, and schools irrespective of low or high starting points. By comparison, the procedures for conventional paper-and-pencil tests are cumbersome, expensive, time-consuming, and poorly protected against cheating.

Finally, the greatest advantage of the computer-managed tests is that they can be given up to four times a year to individual students and groups at a cost lower than the typical cost of conventional tests, which are usually given only annually. They can easily be given when a transfer or migrant student enters a school during the year, and they cannot easily be compromised by cheating efforts. Just as firms and organizations benefit from more frequent reports of results, principals, teachers, and parents can make use of detailed reports on individual students, classes, teachers, and the school as a whole, say, in September, December, February, and May. Both overall status and value-added reports for each child, classroom, and school as a whole can be prepared for parents, school boards, citizens, and the legislature.

Some large cities and states may have the technical staff and resources to custom build similar tests on their own. It seems likely that for-profit testing companies will adopt some or all of the NWEA features. Alternatively, for a fee, district authorities may custom design assessments for school districts that are aligned with their state's standards.

3. Align formative testing and informal evaluation with state standards

District and school staff can form work groups, organized by grade level and possibly by subject much like those described above, to develop practical classroom assessments to measure weekly or monthly progress of students (Walberg, 2006; Walberg, Haertel, & Gerlach-Downie, S., 1994). These tests need not have the length and high reliability of summative tests, but they can reveal rough and ready estimates of student strengths and weaknesses with respect to AYP on the state standards. Teachers and administrators can gear their efforts in part on the results of such formative tests.

Some of the ways such assessment can be accomplished are traditional practices that work. In using direct instruction, for example, astute teachers may watch the demeanor of students to see if they look bored, enthusiastic, or puzzled. They can raise questions and check understanding. They can ask students to write on black boards to solve problems, have them explain their work, and correct faulty reasoning. Teachers can assign seatwork and circulate to see individual students are making good progress. Homework can be assigned and checked either by the teacher or fellow students.

4. Employ quick feedback from classroom tests to evaluate progress

Many psychological studies (Brophy, 1999; Cawelti, 2004; Walberg, 2006) show that immediate or quick feedback streamlines learning. It can help prevent learners from practicing the wrong things, and it can reward students for accurate responses, mental and physical skills, solid knowledge acquisition, deep understanding, and critical thinking.

Such assessment can quickly inform teachers about which students are falling behind. Unless their problems are remedied, they fall farther and farther behind because they have not mastered the prerequisites for advanced understanding. In reading history, for example, students may not grasp the course of a war without knowing its causes and circumstances; others may have difficulties in grasping decimal fractions before comprehending common fractions.

5. Monitor class and group progress with respect to standards mastery

Just as teachers can inform themselves about individual student progress, they can become knowledgeable about their class as a whole and about NCLB categories of students such as Asians, Blacks, and Hispanics; special education; and free and reduced lunch (Chubb, 2005; Paik, 2007; Taylor, 2006). Of course, the collective progress of individual students determines the schools' aggregated group progress toward meeting AYP. If some groups are making inadequate progress, it behooves staff to concentrate more resources on them as suggested by the next two principles.

6. Re-teach topics and skills for which there is insufficient progress

At least three powerful methods of instruction can readily accommodate re-teaching (Cawelti, 2004; Marzano, Pickering, & Pollock, 2001; Walberg, 2006). Direct instruction can be viewed as traditional or conventional whole-group teaching done well. Since teaching changed very little in the 20th century and may not change substantially in the near future, it is worthwhile knowing how the usual practice can excel. Since it has evolved from ordinary practice, direct teaching is relatively easy to carry out, does not disrupt conventional expectations, and can incorporate teaching various subcomponents such as asking questions.

Scholars do not completely agree on the definition of direct instruction. They may refer to it as explicit, process-product, direct, active, or effective teaching. The earliest reviews emphasized observed traits of teachers including clarity, task orientation, enthusiasm, and flexibility, as well as their tendencies to structure their presentations and occasionally use student ideas. The early summaries of research emphasized systematic sequencing of lessons, including the use of review, the presentation of new content and skills, guided student practice, the use of feedback and correctives, and independent student practice.

Based on later observational and control-group research, reviewers identified six phased functions of explicit teaching: (1) daily homework check, review, and, if necessary, re-teaching; (2) rapid presentation of new content and skills in small steps; (3) guided student practice with close monitoring by teachers; (4) corrective feedback and instructional reinforcement; (5) independent practice in seatwork and homework with high (more than 90%) success rate; and (6) weekly and monthly review (Brophy, 1999; Subotnik & Walberg, 2006).

Following the same evolution of research, reviewers identified the essential elements of "Mastery Learning." Originally conceived by Benjamin Bloom, Mastery Learning combines suitable amounts of time for individual students and behavioral elements of teaching (Walberg, 2006):

- "Cues" show students what is to be learned and explain how to learn it. Cues are more effective with increased clarity, salience, and meaningfulness of explanations and directions provided by teachers, instructional materials, or both. As the learners gain confidence, in ideal circumstances, the salience and numbers of cues can be reduced.

- "Engagement" is the extent to which learners actively and persistently participate until appropriate responses are firmly entrenched in their repertoires. Such participation can be indexed by the extent to which the teacher engages students in overt activity – indicated by absence of irrelevant behavior, concentration on tasks, enthusiastic contributions to group discussion, and lengthy study.

- "Corrective feedback" remedies errors in oral or written responses. In ideal circumstances, students waste little time on incorrect responses, and teachers rapidly detect and remedy difficulties by re-teaching or using alternate methods. When necessary, teachers provide additional time for practice.

- "Reinforcement" is illustrated in the efforts elicited by athletics, games, and other cooperative and competitive activities. Immediate and direct reinforcement make some activities intrinsically rewarding. As emphasized by some theorists, classroom reinforcement may gain efficacy mainly by a rewarding sense of accomplishment or providing knowledge of results.

Formative tests are employed to allocate time and guide reinforcement and corrective feedback. Mastery usually takes additional time, a reported median of 16 percent but up to 97 percent more time than conventional teaching. On the other hand, its effects are large, and, in restructuring schools, some students are likely to require the extra time to attain AYP and eventual proficiency.

Developed by the late Ann Brown and others, "Reciprocal Teaching" is a third approach that can incorporate re-teaching when it appears necessary (Cawelti, 2004; Subotnik & Walberg, 2006). In the 1980s, cognitive psychologists sought teaching methods to encourage "meta-cognition" or "learning to learn." In this approach, learners monitor and manage their evolving knowledge, skills, and understanding with self-management viewed as more important than simple acquisition. Teachers transferred some of the responsibility for explicit teaching functions of planning, allocating time, and review. It turned out that that such self-teaching and self-monitoring of progress fostered learner independence, particularly of more advanced content.

How does reciprocal teaching work? It is not dissimilar to the old saying: "To learn something well, teach it," which encourages learners to coherently organize material in preparation for teaching to make it clear and memorable to themselves and others. One practical way to accomplish this is to ask students to each master separate but inter-related parts of a challenging reading selection and organize it for presentation. They take turns, often in groups of two, in imparting the pertinent features of their part of the text. In reciprocal teaching, students learn planning, structuring, and self-management by assuming the planning and executive control ordinarily exercised by teachers.

Similarly, "comprehension teaching" encourages students to measure their progress toward explicit goals. It can be described as a three-stage process of (1) modeling, where the teacher demonstrates the desired behavior; (2) guided practice, where the students perform with help from the teachers; and (3) application, where the student works independently of the teacher. Learners are encouraged to increase their self-awareness of their own progress and reallocate time for their weak points when necessary. Comprehension teaching encourages students to measure their progress toward explicit goals.

7. Extend learning time for topics and skills that lack sufficient progress

Research on mastery learning suggests that some students within a grade may require five times as much time to attain proficiency as other students (Cawelti, 2004; Subotnik & Walberg, 2006; Topping, 2000). Just as these students may require re-teaching and more intense instruction, they may need considerable extra time as well.

Mastery learning allows for accommodation as does small group instruction and tutoring. Though it would be desirable to advance all students – high, middle, and low achievers – as far as possible, under NCLB, restructuring schools must concentrate on bringing as many students as possible to proficiency. Thus, student groups that are not succeeding may need after-school, Saturday school, and summer school programs.

8. Devote resources to monitoring classroom practice

Another advantage of frequent summative and formative assessment is that individual teachers can ask themselves why progress is being made in some subject areas and not in others (Kamil, Manning, & Walberg, 2002; Marzano, Pickering, & Pollock, 2001). The problem may be one of standards, curriculum, teaching, and assessment alignment, but it may also be instructional problems. As mentioned above, careful formative assessment may reveal the source of the difficulty.

Observations of classroom teaching together with feedback and constructive discussions with other teachers and school and district staff may reveal the difficulty. Teacher task force discussions on specific problems may yield the best results.

9. Devote resources to remedying ineffective classroom practices

If teaching methods are found to be ineffective, obviously, more effective methods and programs are to be recommended. Several are discussed above, and as pointed out in the introduction, a number of useful scientifically based works are available that describe others. Frequent formative and summative assessment and classroom observations of teaching and feedback increase the probability that ineffective practices are caught early and remedied (Marzano, Pickering, & Pollock, 2001; Subotnik & Walberg, 2006).

10. Focus efforts on helping parents to help their children meet standards

In their first 18 years of life, youngsters are in school only eight percent of their total number of hours. The years outside school, particularly the early years, have profound, pervasive, and lasting effects on their learning. It is difficult to overcome cognitive deprivation and the loss of academic stimulation at home before and during the school years. Children from low-income families particularly benefit from early childhood language enrichment. Poor children tend to have reduced depth and breadth in their vocabulary. In addition to encouraging and supervising homework and reducing television viewing, parents can improve academic conditions in the home.

Sizable proportions of young children, especially those in poverty, are behind in language and other skills before they begin school. These children often end up in bilingual and special education programs for the "developmentally challenged" in which they are segregated from other children, and they make poor progress. The origins of their achievement problems can partially be attributed to ineffective programs; however, there are specific parental behaviors observed even before the child begins school that substantially affect a child's reading and other language skills in later school-age years.

Children first develop vocabulary and comprehension skills by listening, particularly to their parents before they begin school. As they gain experience with written language between the first and seventh grades, their reading ability gradually rises to the level of their listening ability. Highly skilled listeners in kindergarten make faster reading progress in the later grades, which leads to a growing ability gap between initially skilled and unskilled readers.

This growing gap in reading skill levels reflects inequalities in socioeconomic status and child-rearing practices. These differences stem from early childhood experience, especially with respect to parent behaviors that motivate children. Studies show that middle-class parents are more likely to hold high expectations for their children's achievement and to be more often engaged with them in promoting it.

Home observations and interviews with parents reveal further differences associated with higher achievement in reading correlated with parental socioeconomic status, such as the parent responsiveness and involvement with the child, kinds of discipline employed, household organization, and providing appropriate play materials. Parent behaviors such as these cause huge and growing gaps in preparation for school and learning to read between children in poverty and those in middle-class homes.

One study reported findings from recordings of preschool children's vocabulary growth during free play. Though vocabulary differences were tiny at 12 to 14 months of age, by age 3, sharp differences emerged, correlated with parents' socioeconomic status. Welfare children had vocabularies of about 500 words, middle/lower SES children about 700, and higher SES children had vocabularies of about 1,100 words, more than twice that of welfare children.

Parents of higher socioeconomic status spent more minutes per hour interacting with their children and spoke to them more frequently. On average, higher SES parents spoke about 2,000 words per hour to their children; welfare parents, only about 500. By age 4, "an average child in a professional family would have accumulated experience with almost 45 million words, an average child in a working-class family would have accumulated experience with 26 million words, and an average child in a welfare family with 13 million words" (Hart & Risley, p. 198).

Parents of higher socioeconomic status, moreover, used "more different words, more multi-clause sentences, more past and future verb tenses, more declaratives, and more questions of all kinds. The professional parents also gave their children more affirmative feedback and responded to them more often each hour they were together" (Hart & Risley, 1995, pp. 123-124). By age 4, children of professionally employed parents are encouraged with positive feedback 750,000 times, about 6 times as often as children of welfare parents. The welfare parents, on the other hand, had discouraged their children with negative feedback about 275,000 times, about 2.2 times the amount employed by higher income parents. Such parenting behaviors predicted about 60 percent of the variation in vocabulary growth and use by 3-year-olds.

Entwisle and Alexander (1993) concluded that differences in exposure to vocabulary and elaborate use of language compound at ages 5 and 6, when children from low-income families enter school. Not only do children from lower income families lack vocabulary and other skills, but they must accommodate to educational institutions with "middle-class" norms and values. In their words:

> Many minority and disadvantaged children cross the first-grade threshold lacking competencies and habits of conduct that are required by the school...The conventions of the school, with its achievement orientation, its expectation that children will stay on task and work independently without close monitoring, its tight schedule of moving from lesson to lesson, its use of "network" English, its insistence on punctuality, and its evaluation of children in terms of what they can do instead of who they are, all can be daunting. (p. 405)

Lower SES children are more often identified by their kindergarten teachers as being at-risk for serious academic or adjustment problems; they are absent more in the first grade; and they receive lower teacher ratings on behaviors related to school adjustment such as interest/participation and attention span/restlessness (the latter two strongly predict later academic progress; Entwisle & Alexander, 1993, p. 407).

Students who are behind at the beginning of schooling or slow to start usually learn at a slower rate; those who start ahead gain at a faster rate, which results in what has been called cumulative advantage or the "Matthew effect" of the academically rich getting richer (Walberg & Tsai, 1984), after the passage in chapter 25 of Matthew in the Bible. These effects are pervasive in school learning, including the development of reading comprehension and verbal literacy. Ironically, although improved instructional programs may benefit all students, they may confer greater advantages on those who are initially advantaged. For this reason, the first six years of life and the "curriculum of the home" are decisive influences on academic learning.

The "curriculum of the home" can be much more predictive of academic learning than the family's socioeconomic status (Marzano, Pickering, & Pollock, 2001; Redding, 2000, 2006). A productive and stimulating home environment includes (1) informed parent–child conversations about school and everyday events; (2) encouragement and discussion of leisure reading; (3) monitoring, discussion, and guidance of television viewing and peer activities; (4) deferral of immediate gratification to accomplish long term goals; (5) expressions of affection and interest in the child's academic and other progress as a person; and perhaps, among such efforts, (6) laughter and spontaneity.

Case studies of poor inner-city Chicago families, for example, showed the children who succeeded in school had parents who emphasized and supported their children's academic efforts, encouraged them to read, and interceded on their behalf at school. Many statistical studies show that indexes of such parent behaviors predict children's academic achievement much better than socioeconomic status and poverty. Such cooperative efforts by parents and educators to modify alterable academically stimulating conditions in the home have had beneficial effects on learning for both older and younger students.

Therefore, educators can help parents, including those in poor families, to help their children, at home and in their communities. Several works referenced in the introduction to this module describe educator-induced techniques that help parents to academically stimulate their children. These have been offered by educators in summers and before, during, and after regular school hours during the academic year. Thus, teachers can help parents to learn and practice the various aspects of the curriculum of the home discussed above.

Conclusion

Syntheses of experimental, quasi-experimental, correlational, and observational studies of classrooms and homes reveal a number of instruction and assessment principles that work well, and most are neither unusual nor costly; none defy common sense. Three generalizations underlie these principles:

For effective attainment of ends, align means with ends and the measurement of progress towards the ends. In this case, curriculum, instruction, and assessment must flow from NCLB-required state standards.

Based on monitoring of assessment data, allocate resources, effort, and time to activities that help all NCLB-student groups cross the proficiency line. This implies increasing the amount and the intensity or quality of instruction for students, topics, and grade levels that are failing to make AYP.

To extend academic time, recruit parents and help them to stimulate their children at home and to communicate constructively and often with their child's teachers and other school staff.

References

Brophy, J. (1999). *Teaching.* Geneva, Switzerland: United Nations Educational, Scientific, and Cultural Organization. Retrieved Fall 2006 from http://www.ibe.unesco.org/publications/practices.htm

Cawelti, G. (Ed.). (2004). *Handbook of research on improving student achievement.* Arlington, VA: Educational Research Service.

Chubb, J. E. (Ed.). (2005). *Within our reach: How America can educate every child.* New York: Rowman & Littlefield.

Entwisle, D. R., & Alexander, K. L. (1993). Entry into school: The beginning school transition and educational stratification in the United States. *Annual Review of Sociology, 19,* 401-423.

Hart, B., & Risley, T. R. (1955). *Meaningful differences in the everyday experience of young American children.* Baltimore, MD: Paul H. Brooks.

Just for Kids. (n.d.). *Best practices of high-performing school systems.* Retrieved Fall 2006 from http://www.just4kids.org/bestpractice/evidence_finder.cfm?sub=tools

Kamil, M. L., Manning, J. B., & Walberg, H. J. (2002). *Successful reading instruction.* Greenwich, CT: Information Age Publishing.

Marzano, R. J., Pickering, D. J., & Pollock, J. E. (2001). *Classroom instruction that works: Research-based strategies for increasing student achievement.* Alexandria, VA: Association for Supervision and Curriculum Development.

Paik, S. J. & Walberg, H. J. (2007). *Narrowing the achievement gap: Strategies for educating Latino, Black, and Asian students.* New York: Springer.

Pang, E. S., Muaka, A., Bernhardt, E. B., & Kamil, M. L. (2003). *Teaching reading.* Geneva, Switzerland: United Nations Educational, Scientific, and Cultural Organization. Retrieved Fall 2006 from http://www.ibe.unesco.org/publications/practices.htm

Redding, S. (2000). *Parents and learning.* Geneva, Switzerland: United Nations Educational, Scientific, and Cultural Organization. Retrieved Fall 2006 from http://www.ibe.unesco.org/publications/practices.htm

Redding, S. (2006) *The Mega System: Deciding. Learning. Connecting. A handbook for continuous improvement within a community of the school.* Lincoln, IL: Academic Development Institute.

Shih, C. S., & Weekly, D. E. (2006). *Using new media.* Geneva, Switzerland: United Nations International Bureau of Education. Retrieved Fall 2006 from http://www.ibe.unesco.org/publications/EducationalPracticesSeriesPdf/Practice_15.pdf

Subotnik, R. F., & Walberg, H. J. (2006). *The scientific basis of educational productivity.* Greenwich, CT: Information Age Publishing.

Taylor, R. D. (Ed.). (2006). *Addressing the achievement gap: Findings and applications.* Greenwich, CT: Information Age Publishing.

Topping, K. (2000). *Tutoring.* Geneva, Switzerland: United Nations Educational, Scientific, and Cultural Organization. Retrieved Fall 2006 from http://www.ibe.unesco.org/publications/practices.htm

Walberg, H. J., Haertel, G. D., Gerlach-Downie, S. (1994). *Assessment reform: Challenges and opportunities.* Bloomington, IN: Phi Delta Kappa Educational Foundation.

Walberg, H. J., & Tsai, S.-L. (1984). Matthew effects in education. *American Educational Research Journal, 20,* 359-374.
Wallace, T., Starhia, W. E., & Walberg, H. J. (2004). *Teaching speaking, listening, and writing.* Geneva, Switzerland: United Nations Educational, Scientific, and Cultural Organization. Retrieved Fall 2006 from http://www.ibe.unesco.org/publications/practices.htm.

About the Author

Herbert J. Walberg serves as Chief Scientific Advisor to the Center on Innovation & Improvement. He has retired from 38 years of teaching at Harvard University and the University of Illinois at Chicago. He served as coordinator of a book-conference series on educational improvement at the Laboratory for Student Success (LSS) – a series that focused on improving achievement among at-risk urban and rural children. He served as a founding member and chair of the Design and Analysis Committee of the National Assessment Governing Board, referred to as "the national school board," given its mission to set education standards for U.S. students and measure progress in achieving them. He is now Distinguished Visiting Fellow at the Stanford University Hoover Institution. He is a founding fellow of the International Academy of Education, headquartered in Brussels, for which he edits a booklet series on effective educational practices distributed by the UNESCO International Bureau of Education. This work continues his longstanding interests in providing evidence-based practical information to policymakers and educators. He has given invited lectures in Australia, Belgium, China, England, France, Germany, Italy, Israel, Japan, the Netherlands, South Africa, Sweden, Taiwan, Venezuela, and the United States to educators and policymakers on subjects including standards, accountability, and educational improvement.

6. Systems for Improved Teaching and Learning

Sam Redding

To implement and sustain substantially improved teaching and learning in the restructured school, systems must be in place to enable the people attached to the school to competently fulfill their roles and achieve clear goals, especially improved student learning.

Abstract

This module outlines systems for initiating and monitoring significant instructional change in a restructured school. The principles of effective instructional practice are tied to underlying research and made part of a system of continuous improvement, including instructional planning, professional development, and teacher evaluation. Team responsibility for instructional planning, scrutiny of student learning outcomes, and adjustments in course build teacher competence and dedication to the substantial improvement required under restructuring.

Introduction

Restructuring a school is akin to shaking an ailing tree by its roots and replanting it in richer soil. Restructuring is not cosmetic pruning. Restructuring is not increased application of fertilizer. When a school arrives at the point where restructuring is necessary, the nutrients of expert guidance and professional development have already been applied in most cases. Incremental school improvement has been attempted. The time has arrived for something more dra-

Handbook on Restructuring and Substantial School Improvement
Copyright © 2007 by Information Age Publishing and The Academic Development Institute
All rights of reproduction in any form reserved.

matic in order to achieve significant and sustained growth in student learning. The district develops a plan to restructure the school, to significantly change the way it is organized and governed. The school is shaken by the roots.

Once the roots have been shaken in a restructured school, what then? Once the school has been reorganized, staff replaced perhaps, turnaround experts engaged, curriculum swapped, what happens on the next day? What is the richer soil that surrounds the shaken and replanted roots? How does the restructured school set itself on a course of continuous improvement without the word "continuous" becoming synonymous with plodding? The restructured school must make a quick shift in emphasis from structural reconfiguration to microscopic examination of each student's learning and careful attention to each staff member's performance.

First the school must be sure the new soil is rich, the conditions right for the school's own staff to perform at a higher level and to sustain, even accelerate, the systemic improvement. While the school will continue to receive oversight and assistance from beyond its walls, from the district for sure and possibly from the state and external consultants, the community of people intimately attached to that one school, must take charge of the learning enterprise in order to improve learning outcomes for the children in their midst. Administrators, support staff, teachers, parents, and the students themselves must see life in the restructured school in a new light, one that clearly illuminates each of their interrelated and mutually significant roles and responsibilities.

On the day after the restructuring plan has been enacted, life begins anew for the people attached to the school. The mental energy that has been channeled into reconceptualizing the school's organizational structure is now redirected to the concerted activities of all the players and to each student's learning. How is the school experience different now for Susie in her third-grade reading class? For Johnny in ninth-grade algebra? How do Susie's teachers now relate more purposefully to one another? How do Johnny's parents now understand their role in their son's school success? How do Susie and Johnny shoulder the higher expectations placed on them, assume increased responsibility for their learning, and view their teachers and parents as partners in their learning? How does the principal foster both the vision and the technical know-how to hold all the stars in this night sky together in a bright and coherent constellation?

Sashkin and Egermeier (1993) suggest that a focus on accountability and restructuring creates changes in roles, rules, and relationships for students, teachers, parents, administrators, central office staff, and the state, all aimed now with greater urgency on improving student outcomes. Fullan (2001) cautions that restructuring is no more than organizational tinkering unless it is accompanied by reculturing – changes in the norms, values, incentives, skills, and relationships among the people who constitute the school. Schlecty (1990) warns that restructuring does not automatically or even inevitably make a difference in teaching and learning. Beliefs, values, and knowledge must change, meaning that human and social capital must increase and become sharply focused on learning. Once the restructuring plan is in place, the school culture must change, and it must change in quick order, with the consequences apparent in the classroom and in the relationships among the constituents of the school community. A change in school culture comes not from exhortation but from coherent systems of improvement, competently designed and executed (Redding, 2006).

Principles

1. Establish a team structure with specific duties and time for instructional planning

Marzano (2003) points out that leadership should not reside with one individual; a team approach to planning and decision making allows for distributive leadership. Planning and decision making within the restructured school require *teams*, *time*, and *access to timely information*. That is, decision-making groups must be organized and given time to plan and monitor the parts of the system for which they are responsible. This is an immense challenge in most schools, where teachers are available for very little time beyond the hours for which they are responsible for teaching and supervising students. Finding time for a group of teachers to meet is not easy, but essential. Different groups or teams of school personnel have different needs for the amount and distribution of time required for them to attend to their responsibilities. Additional time is needed for professional development; professional development should be directly tied to classroom observations and analysis of student learning data.

A basic structure for team planning, work, and decision making includes a Leadership Team, Instructional Teams, and a team focused on the family-school connection (such as a School Community Council). The Leadership Team is headed by the principal and includes teachers and other key staff. In order to facilitate communication and coordination among the grade levels and departments of the school, a typical Leadership Team is comprised of the principal and team leaders from the Instructional Teams (grade level or subject area teams). The Leadership Team may also function as the School Improvement Team, with parent members attending meetings scheduled for purposes of reviewing and amending the school improvement plan. Instructional Teams are manageable groupings of teachers by grade level or subject area who meet to develop instructional strategies aligned to the standards-based curriculum and to monitor the progress of the students in the grade levels or subject area for which the team is responsible. A School Community Council is comprised of the principal, counselor, social worker, teachers, and parents (typical configuration), with parents constituting the majority of the membership. The School Community Council advises, plans, and assists with matters related to the school-home compact, homework, open houses, parent-teacher conferences, school-home communication, and parent education (including training and information about learning standards and the parents' role in supporting children's learning at home).

2. Focus the principal's role on building leadership capacity, achieving learning goals, and improving instruction

The leadership characteristics necessary in reform, especially reform of the "turnaround" variety, differ from those of the manager in a more stable situation of continuous school improvement. Managerial aspects of the job do not fade away, but the principal in a restructured school is a change agent more than a manager.

Lambert (2000) portrays the principal as the fire carrier for the school's vision, the central character in instructional planning, and a collaborator who brings teachers and even parents into discussions about the school's operation. The principal is the focus keeper, consistently pointing to improved student learning as the central goal of the school. The principal sets the climate of high expectations for student achievement and sees that teams function effectively.

Blasé and Kirby (2000) identified three leader characteristics as critical to building personal relationships that are conducive to effective reform efforts: (1) optimism, (2) honesty, and (3) consideration. Optimism provides hope during the difficult times that inevitably come with change initiatives. It is defined as the power of non-negative thinking. The leader acknowledges obstacles but does not portray them as insurmountable. Honesty is characterized by truthfulness, but also by congruence between words and actions. To sustain a change effort, teachers and parents must have a sense that what they are told is accurate and that there are no important things occurring about which they are not informed. Consideration is a trait that refers to "people orientation" or a concern for people, especially a concern for each person. Considerate principals, for example, express interest in their teachers' lives.

Schmoker (1996) encourages schools to set small, measurable goals that can be achieved monthly, quarterly, or annually. Small, measurable successes are the seeds of large-scale success, and can release optimism and enthusiasm, or "zest" as Schaffer (1988) calls it. A teaching staff can use this zest to maintain energy for reaching further goals. So, a principal's task is to help the instructional staff focus the goals on both short-term and long-term student achievement.

3. Engage teachers in aligning instruction with standards and benchmarks

In an effective system, teachers, working in teams, build the taught curriculum from learning standards, curriculum guides, and a variety of resources, including textbooks, other commercial materials, and teacher-created activities and materials. Instructional Teams organize the curriculum into unit plans that guide instruction for all students and for each student. The unit plans assure that students master standards-based objectives and also provide opportunities for enhanced learning.

A unit of instruction is typically three to six weeks of work within a subject area for a particular grade level or course sequence. To pool teacher expertise and secure a guaranteed, taught curriculum, an Instructional Team can develop a plan for each unit. The plan is shared by all the teachers who teach that subject and grade level. The alignment process serves two related purposes: It serves as a check on guide/text/test congruence, and it provides teachers with an organizational structure for their own planning (Glatthorn, 1995).

The unit plan is developed by the Instructional Team to define a unit of instruction and outline the standards and target objectives (typically grade level) addressed in the unit of instruction.

The Instructional Team:

1. Determines the concepts, principles, and skills that will be covered within the unit.
2. Identifies the standards/benchmarks that apply to the grade level and unit topic.
3. Develops all objectives that clearly align to the selected standards/benchmarks.
4. Arranges the objectives in sequential order.
5. Determines the best objective descriptors.
6. Considers the most appropriate elements for mastery and constructs criteria for mastery.
7. Develops pre/post-test items that are clear and specific and would provide evidence of mastery consistent with the criteria established.

Examples of Objectives in a Unit Plan

Target Objective: The student will be able to name the four primary directions on a navigational compass. (This is an objective at the level of general knowledge.)

Criteria for Mastery: Given a blank compass face, the student will write the name of the four primary directions in the correct locations.

Pre-test/Post-test Item: Mark the four primary directions on the blank compass face.

Prerequisite Objective: The student will be able to identify the four primary directions on a navigational compass by matching the points to a list of North, South, East, West. (This is an objective at the level of general knowledge.)

Enhanced Objective: The student will be able to write a short paragraph explaining the positions of the four primary directions on a navigational compass. (This is an objective at the comprehension level.)

4. Engage teachers in assessing and monitoring student mastery

A unit test is an assessment device, aligned with each standards-based objective covered in the unit, and administered to all students before and after the unit of instruction (or smaller parts of the unit). The pre-test and post-test are the *same* test, or parallel items for the same objectives, given at the beginning and end of a unit. In some cases, especially in the lower grades, the unit test is divided into a series of smaller tests, given before and after instruction in the objectives covered on the smaller test. Unit tests are constructed to give teachers a good idea of a student's current level of mastery of the objectives without taking a great amount of time to administer. A unit test need not be a pencil and paper test, especially in the lower grades, but is a way for the teacher to specifically check each student's mastery of each objective in a manner that is not time consuming.

5. Engage teachers in differentiating and aligning learning activities

Learning activities, the assignments given to each student targeted to that student's level of mastery, should be carefully aligned with the objectives included in the unit plan to provide a variety of ways for a student to achieve mastery as evidenced in *both* the successful completion of the learning activities and correct responses on the unit post-test. An Instructional Team's unit plans include a description of each leveled and differentiated learning activity, the standards-based objectives associated with it, and criteria for mastery. These activities become arrows in the teacher's quiver of instructional options for each student.

The unit plan aligns the curriculum to standards and benchmarks. The next step is to align the curriculum to instruction. This is where the real fun begins – teachers sharing their most successful instructional strategies for meeting each objective in the unit of instruction. Unit plans level each objective into three tiers – target, enhanced, and prerequisite. The unit plans also differentiate learning activities among various modes of instruction – whole-class instruction, independent work, small-group and center-based activities, and homework. The activity instructions provide the detail that enables any teacher to use the learning activity, and also become a means of explaining the activity to students.

6. Assess student learning frequently with standards-based assessments

Assessment is the process of testing (written, verbal, or by examination of work) to see: (1) what a student knows and can do, and (2) patterns of strengths and weakness in what a group of students knows and can do. Assessment includes: (1) diagnostic-prescriptive assessments, such as unit pre-tests and post-tests, used by teachers and teams; (2) embedded assessments that are part of learning activities by which the teacher determines mastery of objectives by the student's successful completion of the activity; (3) periodic assessments, such as those provided by testing firms or developed by the district or school to gauge student mastery of standards-based objectives at several points through the school year; and 4) annual assessments such as state standards assessments and standardized achievement tests.

7. Expect and monitor sound instruction in a variety of modes

The most widely replicated findings concerning the characteristics of teachers who elicit strong achievement score gains are:

1. **Teacher Expectation/Role Definition/Sense of Efficacy:** Teachers accept responsibility for teaching their students. They believe that students are capable of learning. They re-teach if necessary, and alter materials as needed.
2. **Student Opportunity to Learn:** Teachers allocate most of their available time to instruction, not non-academic activities, and learning activities are carefully aligned to standards.
3. **Classroom Management and Organization:** Teachers organize their learning environments and use group management approaches effectively to maximize time students spend engaged in lessons.

4. **Curriculum Pacing:** Teachers move through the curriculum rapidly but in small steps that minimize student frustration and allow continuous progress.

5. **Active Teaching (sometimes called Direct Instruction):** Teachers actively instruct, demonstrating skills, explaining concepts, conducting participatory activities, reviewing when necessary. They teach their students rather than expecting them to learn mostly from curriculum materials. They do not just stress facts or skills, they also emphasize concepts and understanding.

6. **Teaching to Mastery:** Following active instruction, teachers provide opportunities for students to practice and apply learning. They monitor each student's progress and provide feedback and remedial instruction as needed, making sure students achieve mastery.

7. **A Supportive Learning Environment:** In addition to their strong academic focus, these teachers maintain pleasant, friendly classrooms and are perceived as enthusiastic, supportive instructors.

(Brophy & Good, 1986; Good, 1996; Reynolds, 1992; Waxman & Walberg, 1991)

An analysis of quality of instruction (Walberg, 1984; Wang, Haertel, & Walberg, 1993) finds evidence of the strength of particular instructional elements, mastery learning techniques, direct instruction, and graded homework. Techniques employed during teacher-directed instruction have demonstrated impressive power (effect sizes) in studies of student learning. Cues, for example, are especially effective in activating prior knowledge and alerting students to important information (Walberg & Lai, 1999). Connecting to prior knowledge is not only helpful in organizing new learning, but increases students' interest in the topic (Alexander, Kulikowich, & Schulze, 1994). Advance organizers, first popularized by psychologist David Ausubel (1968), provide scaffolding for the incorporation of new material to be introduced within the next 20 minutes or so. Advance organizers take such forms as visual graphics, lists, and statements abstracting the material. Simply describing the new content (expository advance organizer) is the most effective type of advance organizer, but other forms (narrative – brief presentation in story form, skimming – quick preview of text, and illustrated – use of visuals) are also effective (Stone, 1983). Internal summaries and the rule-example-rule approach have demonstrated their power in enhancing learning (Rosenshine, 1968). The agile teacher who is able to articulate clear goals and expectations for the lesson and make wise decisions in the use of various instructional techniques is key to teacher-directed instruction (Good & Brophy, 2000).

Teacher-directed, small-group instruction is an effective follow-up to the whole-class presentation, enabling the teacher to focus instructional attention on the particular requirements of homogeneous groups of students. The group-ings should be fluid, rearranged frequently in response to particular learning needs. Students should not be clustered in other ways – such as seating ar-rangements – that appear to solidify group membership and "label" members. Because groups are formed to address particular learning needs, they will vary from time to time in number of members and in the time devoted to them (Good & Brophy, 2000). Small groups may also be employed for student-directed learning, with instructions provided by the teacher, and are especially effective for cooperative learning and peer-to-peer learning.

More and more, technology is used to individualize instruction, provide a well-organized presentation of material, offer feedback, and allow students to progress at their own rate. Computer-based instruction is successful when the program is carefully aligned with the same standards and objectives that the teacher is addressing within the designated unit of instruction. This requires the teacher to know the content of the computer program and to use it in concert with other modes of instruction. It also requires that the teacher check for mastery of objectives independent of the program's validation of mastery. When a computer program is successful, students are engaged, on task, and comfortable with the program and its navigation. The teacher travels about the room to assist students and monitor their work. When a student is in need of assistance from the teacher, the teacher provides curriculum-related activities to avoid "down time." In terms of classroom management, the students are taught to make orderly transitions to and from their computer stations.

With technology-assisted instruction, the teacher uses computers and other technology tools as a seamless part of the learning activity. Students use word processing programs to write and edit their written work. They develop projects with presentation software. They use the internet as a source of information. All this requires clear direction to gather, organize, and present information. To make technology-assisted instruction fruitful, teachers must be trained in the use of the software and must be supported in integrating the technology into the routine of instruction. Technology can also be a great asset to teachers in their recordkeeping.

8. Expect and monitor sound homework practices and communication with parents

Research has long established the strong influence of a student's home envi-ronment on that student's success in school. We now have significant, new re-search that shows that schools can improve their students' learning by engaging parents in ways that directly relate to their children's academic progress, main-taining a consistent message of what is expected of parents, and reaching parents directly, personally, and with a trusting approach (Epstein, 1995; Henderson & Mapp, 2002; Patrikakou, Weissburg, Redding, & Walberg, 2005; Patrikakou, Weissberg, & Rubenstein, 1999; Redding, 2000). Homework is a primary point of interface between the school and the home, and parents are best able to support the school's purposes for homework when they understand what is expected of students and their role in monitoring their children's homework. Consistency from teacher to teacher and across grade levels and subjects contributes to teachers,' parents,' and students' understanding of the school's purposes for homework and also reinforces students' formation of independent study habits. Homework should be used primarily for practice and mastery rather than introduction of new learning. Homework is most effective when graded, corrected, and promptly returned. Building the student's habits of independent study through regular assignment of homework is the key; the total amount of time devoted to homework is less important, although the amount of time should escalate gradually through the grade levels.

9. Expect and monitor sound classroom management

A meta-analysis of 28 factors that affect school learning (Wang, Haertel, & Walberg, 1993) found that the single most powerful factor is classroom management – the way the teacher organizes and manages the complex variables of curriculum, time, space, and interaction with students. Classroom management is evidenced in the teacher's "withitness," the learner's accountability for learning, the clear procedures in the classroom, and the way the teacher mixes whole-class instruction, small-group instruction, and individual instruction.

Consistent reinforcement of classroom rules and procedures is key to classroom management (Emmer et al., 1984; Evertson et al., 1984). Rules and procedures are posted in the classroom, and students are reminded of them and learn to operate according to them. The effective teacher "teaches" classroom procedures in a positive way rather than relying solely on correction of violations. Frequently resorting to correction and punishment is a sign of inadequate classroom management methods, but consistent enforcement of rules and procedures is a necessity (Stage & Quiroz, 1997).

Teacher "withitness" is described by Brophy (1996) as the teacher being "aware of what is happening in all parts of the classroom at all times…by continuously scanning the classroom, even when working with small groups or individuals. Also [the teacher demonstrates]…this withitness by intervening promptly and accurately when inappropriate behavior threatens to become disruptive" (p. 11). The way a teacher plans, organizes, manages, and watches over the classroom determines the prevailing "culture." Students adopt the ethos of the classroom culture, responding to what the teacher has created and to the way the teacher behaves.

10. Align classroom observations with evaluation criteria and professional development

Professional development should parallel the school improvement plan and evidence of research-based practices in the classroom as determined by systematic classroom observations by the principal and by peers. When the school improvement plan calls for new expertise to enable the school to move in a new direction or to address a particular problem, professional development is a means for elevating the skill and knowledge of administrators, teachers, and staff. When classroom observations by the principal or other teachers (as in peer observation and collegial learning) indicate a general need for improvement across the faculty, well-planned professional development is a way to improve. When classroom observations by the principal or another teacher show an individual teacher's areas that need improvement, that teacher's personal development plan can include training or coaching to assist the teacher in the area of need.

The research-based teaching practices described in principles 7, 8, and 9 above (and listed as indicators in another module in this handbook), provide the elements of a classroom observation instrument. The principal or another teacher would meet with the observed teacher before the observation to review the indicators and again after the observation to discuss the observer's impressions. The teacher and the observer then create or update a professional development plan for the teacher, listing: (a) observed strengths and ways the teacher might share his/her expertise with other teachers, and (b) areas that need improvement and steps toward improvement. The observer assists the teacher in carrying out these next steps.

Continuous improvement of each teacher's skills is achieved through a variety of means including whole-faculty workshops, consultations with Instructional Teams, the principal's work with individual teachers and with teams, and through collegial learning – teacher to teacher (including peer observations, study groups, coaching, and mentoring). While teacher evaluation is something apart from professional development, evaluation should include examination of the teacher's proficiency with the same indicators used to plan professional development for each individual teacher and for the faculty as whole.

Conclusion

A restructuring plan, even restructuring itself, does not ensure substantial and sustained improvement in teaching and learning. Systems must be put in place to tend to the day-to-day work in the school. These systems can be maintained by school-based teams, with leadership focused sharply on classroom instruction and assessed student learning. The team structure enables teachers to systematically align their instruction to standards, individualize their instruction for each student, share their strategies, and assess the effectivess of their methods. Professional development should track patterns of individual and faculty strength and weakness determined by classroom observations by administrators and peers. Thus instructional planning, teaching and learning, assessment of student learning, and professional development become parts of a system of continuous improvement that is able to sustain the early gains that restructuring is intended to produce.

References

Alexander, P. A., Kulikowich, J. M., & Schulze, S. K. (1994). How subject matter knowledge affects recall and interest. *American Educational Research Journal, 31*(2), 313-337.

Ausubel, D. (1968). *Educational psychology: A cognitive view.* New York: Holt, Rinehart & Winston.

Blasé, J., & Kirby, P. C. (2000). *Bringing out the best in teachers: What effective principals do* (2nd ed.). Thousand Oaks, CA: Corwin Press.

Brophy, J. E. (1996). *Teaching problem students.* New York: Guilford.

Brophy, J. E., & Good, T. G. (1986). Teacher behavior and student achievement. In M. Wittrock (Ed.), *Handbook of research in teaching* (3rd ed., pp. 328–375). New York: Macmillan.

Emmer, E. T., Evertson, C. M., Sanford, J. P., Clements, B. S., & Worsham, M. E. (1984). *Classroom management for secondary teachers.* Englewood Cliffs, NJ: Prentice-Hall.

Epstein, J. L. (1995). School/family/community partnerships: Caring for the children we share. *Phi Delta Kappan, 76*(9), 701-712.

Evertson, C. M., Emmer, E. T., Clements, B. S., Sanford, J. P., & Worsham, M. E. (1984). *Classroom management for elementary teachers.* Englewood Cliffs, NJ: Prentice-Hall.

Fullan, M. (2001). *Leading in a culture of change.* San Francisco: Jossey-Bass.

Glatthorn, A. (1995). *Developing a quality curriculum.* Alexandria, VA: Association for Supervision and Curriculum Development.

Good, T. (1996). Teacher effectiveness and teacher evaluation. In J. Sikula, T. Buttery, & E. Guyton (Eds.), *Handbook of research on teacher education* (2nd ed., pp. 617-665). New York: MacMillan.

Good, T. L., & Brophy, J. E. (2000). *Looking in classrooms* (8th ed.). New York: Addison Wesley Longman.

Henderson, A., & Mapp. K. (2002). *A new wave of evidence: The impact of school, family, and community connections on student achievement.* Austin, TX: Southwest Educational Development Laboratory.

Lambert, L. (2003). *Leadership capacity for lasting school improvement.* Alexandria, VA: Association for Supervision and Curriculum Development.

Marzano, R. (2003). *What works in schools: Translating research into action.* Alexandria, VA: Association for Supervision and Curriculum Development.

Patrikakou, E. N., Weissberg, R. P., Redding, S., & Walberg, H. J., (2005). *School-family partnerships for children's success.* New York: Teachers College Press.

Patrikakou, E. N., Weissberg, R. P., & Rubenstein, M. (1999). School-family partnerships. In A. J. Reynolds, H. J. Walberg, & R. P. Weissberg (Eds.), *Promoting positive outcomes* (pp. 95-127). Washington, DC: Child Welfare League of America.

Redding, S. (2000). *Parents and learning.* Geneva: UNESCO Publications.

Redding, S. (2006). *The Mega System: Deciding. Learning. Connecting. A handbook for continuous improvement within a community of the school.* Lincoln, IL: Academic Development Institute.

Reynolds, A. (1992). What is competent beginning teaching? A review of the literature. *Review of Educational Research, 62,* 1-35.

Rosenshine, B. (1968). To explain: A review of research. *Educational Leadership, 26,* 275-280.

Sashkin, M., & Egermeier, J. (1993). *School change models and processes: A review and synthesis of research and practice.* Washington, DC: U.S. Government Printing Office. (ERIC Document Reproduction Service No. 351 757)

Schaffer, R. H. (1988). *The breakthrough strategy: Using short-term successes to build the high-performance organization.* New York: Harper Business.

Schlechty, P. C. (1990). *Schools for the 21ˢᵗ century.* San Francisco: Jossey-Bass.

Schmoker, M. (1996). *Results: The key to continuous school improvement.* Alexandria, VA: Association for Supervision and Curriculum Development.

Stage, S. A., & Quiroz, D. R. (1997). A meta-analysis of interventions to decrease disruptive classroom behavior in public education settings. *School Psychology Review, 26*(3), 333-368.

Stone, C. L. (1983). A meta-analysis of advanced organizer studies. *Journal of Experimental Education, 51*(7), 194-199.

Walberg, H. J. (1984). Improving the productivity of America's schools. *Educational Leadership, 41*(8), 19-27.

Walberg, H. J., & Lai, J.-S. (1999). Meta-analytic effects for policy. In G. J. Cizek (Ed.), *Handbook of educational policy* (pp. 419-453). San Diego, CA: Academic Press.

Wang, M. C., Haertel, G. D., & Walberg, H. J. (1993). Toward a knowledge base for school learning. *Review of Educational Research, 63,* 249-294.

Waxman, H. C., & Walberg, H. J. (Eds.). (1991). *Effective teaching: Current research.* Berkeley, CA: McCutchan.

See Also: *The Mega System* at http://www.adi.org/mega/ and other resources on school improvement and restructuring at www.centerii.org

About the Author

Sam Redding is Director of the Center on Innovation & Improvement. Since 1984 he has served as the Executive Director of the Academic Development Institute (ADI). He has been executive editor of the *School Community Journal* since 1991 and was a senior research associate of the Laboratory for Student Success (LSS) at Temple University from 1995 to 2005. He has edited three books on family-school relationships, written a book on school improvement, and written in the areas of school management, school improvement, and factors affecting school learning. He has served on a variety of state committees, including the standards-writing committee for the Illinois State Board of Education; the Positive Behavioral Interventions & Supports (PBIS) Leadership Team and the ISBE Parent Leadership Team; and the Collaborative for Academic, Social, and Emotional Learning. He has served on various civic boards, as well as the boards of the Effective Schools Institute and Superintendency Institute. Sam has worked directly with more than 40 districts in comprehensive school reform, consulting with their administration, training teachers, and establishing systems for tracking student learning data. He holds a doctorate in Educational Administration from Illinois State University, master's degrees in both Psychology and English, and is a graduate of Harvard's Institute for Educational Management.

7. Indicators of Successful Restructuring

Sam Redding

A restructuring plan's success depends upon district and school collaboration and focus, engagement of parents and the broader community, and disciplined, competent implementation.

Abstract

A restructuring plan must ultimately impact the way the school operates in significant ways, especially in the teaching and learning enterprises. The checklists of indicators in this module are organized into three stages. Stage I addresses the district context and the development of a restructuring plan. Stage II carries the plan into the school, where the faculty aligns the curriculum with instruction and assessment. The items in Stage III form a classroom observation and teacher interview instrument to monitor classroom processes and plan targeted professional development.

Introduction

The *Handbook on Restructuring and Substantial School Improvement* provides a review of research and action-oriented principles for the district and school to apply. This final module in the handbook consolidates the principles into sets of indicators by which district and school teams can periodically assess their progress. While every item may not be appropriate to a particular school's situation, each will provide food for thought in discussing a restructuring or improvement plan. The checklists will also guide school teams through the

Handbook on Restructuring and Substantial School Improvement
Copyright © 2007 by Information Age Publishing and The Academic Development Institute
All rights of reproduction in any form reserved.

implementation of their plans and into continuous school improvement. The sets of items below are arranged sequentially to carry teams through an examination from general (district context) to specific (classroom teaching). The Yes/No dichotomy is an attempt to draw attention to areas of obvious strength and areas in apparent need for improvement. Teams may choose to make more subtle assessments, noting that the item is partially in place but needs bolstering or refinement and then suggesting next steps. Topics and checklists may be used by different teams, from district-level improvement teams to school leadership teams to grade-level teams of teachers, but considering them as a whole is a way to connect all the factors necessary to a systematic approach to school improvement.

The following checklists are available as downloadable forms from www.centerii.org; see the section on Restructuring.

Checklists of Success Indicators

Stage I: District Context and the Restructuring Plan

A. Restructuring the school within a framework of district improvement and support

See modules 1 and 2 in the handbook.

Districts must take the lead in establishing "no excuses" goals and in developing initiatives designed to move all schools toward these. However, it also must be clear that accountability for carrying out these initiatives – and for ensuring every student learns – is in the hands of principals and teachers. To support them and to ensure improvement efforts stay on track, districts should remain actively engaged through efforts such as creation of a curricular focus, intensive development opportunities for staff, monitoring of progress, and provision of resources needed to address intervention needs of individual students. The district engages civic, community, parent, and church groups in its school improvement and restructuring planning.

In an effective district system for school improvement:

Date:_____ Team: _____

Status (check 1)		Success Indicators	Action Required
Yes	No		
		The district includes municipal and civic leaders in school reform and restructuring planning and maintains regular communication with them.	
		The district includes community organizations and churches in school reform and restructuring planning and maintains regular communication with them.	
		The district includes parent organizations in school reform and restructuring planning and maintains regular communication with them.	
		The district provides incentives for staff who work effectively in restructured schools.	
		The district contracts with external service providers for key services in restructured schools.	

Checklist continues

107

A. Restructuring the school within a framework of district improvement and support (continued)

Status (check 1)		Success Indicators	Action Required
Yes	No		
		The district provides schools with technology, training, and support for integrated data collection, reporting, and analysis systems.	
		The district sets district, school, and student subgroup achievement targets.	
		The school board and superintendent present a unified vision for school improvement.	
		The superintendent and other central office staff are accountable for school improvement and student learning outcomes.	
		The district regularly reallocates resources to support school, staff, and instructional improvement.	
		The district ensures that key pieces of *user-friendly* data are available *in a timely fashion* at the district, school, and classroom levels.	
		The district intervenes early when a school is not making adequate progress.	
		The district works with the school to provide early and intensive intervention for students not making progress.	
		The district recruits, trains, supports, and places personnel to competently address the problems of schools in need of improvement.	
		The district allows school leaders reasonable autonomy to do things differently in order to succeed.	

B. Taking the change process into account in choosing the best restructuring option

See module 3 in the handbook.

Restructuring necessitates quick, dramatic change, which requires district support and assessment of each school's strengths and needs. It also requires a plan for resource allocation and evidence-based improvement as well as other conditions of corrective action.

Date:_____ Team: _____

Status (check 1)			
Yes	No	Success Indicators	Action Required
		The district forms district-level and school-level re-structuring teams.	
		The district examines existing school improvement strategies being implemented across the district and determines their value, expanding, modifying, and culling as evidence suggests.	
		The district makes reference to guidance from *What Works When* regarding how to assess what the best NCLB options are given its unique district context.	
		The restructuring options chosen reflect the particular strengths and weaknesses of the restructuring school.	
		The restructuring plan reflects the resources available to ensure its success.	
		The restructuring plan includes both changes in governance and a detailed plan for school improvement in line with requirements associated with NCLB.	
		The restructuring plan includes research-based, field-proven programs, practices, and models.	
		The restructuring plan includes a clear vision of what the school will look like when restructured.	
		An empowered change agent (typically the principal) is appointed to head the restructuring school.	
		The change agent (typically the principal) is skilled in motivating staff and the community, communicating clear expectations, and focusing on improved student learning.	
		The restructuring plan focuses on "quick wins," early successes in improvement.	
		The district is prepared for setbacks, "naysayers," and obstacles on the path to substantial improvement in the restructuring school.	

C. Clarifying district-school expectations

See modules 2 and 3 in the handbook.

The restructuring school needs support from its district and a firm understanding of which decisions are to be made at the district level and which decisions are to be made within the school. District policies and support affect a school's ability to initiate and sustain a system of continuous improvement. Many attempts at school reform have gone awry when the well-intentioned initiatives of the district compete with the earnest efforts of the school for time, resources, and allegiance. The restructuring plan no doubt outlines the district's expectations for the school and may include the district's plans for assistance. A straightforward letter of understanding between the district and the school is a second essential document for a restructured school.

The district-school letter of understanding would include the following:

Date:_____ Team: _____

| Status (check 1) | | | |
Yes	No	Success Indicators	Action Required
		The school reports and documents its progress monthly to the superintendent, and the superintendent reports the school's progress to the school board.	
		The district designates a central office contact person for the school, and that person maintains close communication with the school and an interest in its progress.	
		District and school decision makers meet at least twice a month to discuss the school's progress.	
		District policies and procedures clarify the scope of site-based decision making granted the school and are summarized in this letter.	
		The district provides a cohesive district curriculum guide aligned with state standards or otherwise places curricular expectations on the school summarized in this letter.	
		The district provides the technology, training, and support to facilitate the school's data management needs.	
		Professional development is built into the school schedule by the district, but the school is allowed discretion in selecting training and consultation that fit the requirements of its restructuring plan and its evolving needs.	
		Staff development is built into the schedule for support staff (e.g., aides, clerks, custodians, cooks) as well as classroom teachers.	

D. Establishing a team structure with specific duties and time for instructional planning

See module 6 in the handbook.

Effective instructional practices are tied to underlying research and made part of a system of continuous improvement, including instructional planning, professional development, and teacher evaluation. Team responsibility for instructional planning, scrutiny of student learning outcomes, and adjustments in course build teacher competence and dedication to the substantial improvement required under restructuring.

A system of team-based planning, working, and decision making may be achieved when:

Date:_____ Team: _____

Status (check 1)		Success Indicators	Action Required
Yes	No		
		A team structure is officially incorporated into the school improvement plan and school governance policy.	
		All teams have written statements of purpose and by-laws for their operation.	
		All teams operate with work plans for the year and specific work products to produce.	
		All teams prepare agendas for their meetings.	
		All teams maintain official minutes of their meetings.	
		The principal maintains a file of the agendas, work products, and minutes of all teams.	
		A Leadership Team consisting of the principal, teachers who lead the Instructional Teams, and other key professional staff meets regularly (twice a month or more for an hour each meeting).	
		The Leadership Team serves as a conduit of communication to the faculty and staff.	
		The Leadership Team shares in decisions of real substance pertaining to curriculum, instruction, and professional development.	

Checklist continues

D. Establishing a team structure with specific duties and time for instructional planning (continued)

Status (check 1)		Success Indicators	Action Required
Yes	No		
		The Leadership Team regularly looks at school performance data and aggregated classroom observation data and uses that data to make decisions about school improvement and professional development needs.	
		Teachers are organized into grade-level, grade-level cluster, or subject-area Instructional Teams.	
		Instructional Teams meet regularly (twice a month or more for 45 minutes each meeting) to conduct business.	
		Instructional Teams meet for blocks of time (4 to 6 hour blocks, once a month; whole days before and after the school year) sufficient to develop and refine units of instruction and review student learning data.	
		A School Community Council consisting of the principal, parent facilitator, social worker or counselor, and parents oversees family-school relationships and the curriculum of the home.	
		A majority of the members of the School Community Council are parents of currently enrolled students and are not also employees of the school.	
		The School Community Council meets regularly (twice a month for an hour each meeting).	

E. Focusing the principal's role on building leadership capacity, achieving learning goals, and improving instruction

See modules 4, 5, and 6 in the handbook.

The leadership characteristics necessary in reform, especially reform of the "turnaround" variety, differ from those of the manager in a more stable situation of continuous school improvement. Managerial aspects of the job do not fade away, but the principal in a restructured school is a change agent more than a manager.

The principal's role as tender of the system is compatible with the requirements of a restructured school when the principal:

Date:_____ Team: _____

Status (check 1)		Success Indicators	Action Required
Yes	No		
		Makes sure everyone understands the school's mission, clear goals (short term and long term), and their roles in meeting the goals.	
		Develops the leadership capacity of others in the school.	
		Communicates the likelihood of success based on the plan and hard work.	
		Models and communicates the expectation of improved student learning through commitment, discipline, and careful implementation of sound practices.	
		Participates actively with the school's teams.	
		Keeps a focus on instructional improvement and student learning outcomes.	
		Monitors curriculum and classroom instruction regularly.	
		Spends at least 50% of his/her time working directly with teachers to improve instruction, including classroom observations.	
		Challenges, supports and monitors the correction of unsound teaching practices.	
		Celebrates individual, team, and school successes, especially related to student learning outcomes.	
		Provides incentives for teacher and student accomplishment.	
		Personally engages parents and the community in the improvement process.	
		Offers frequent opportunities for staff and parents to voice constructive critique of the school's progress and suggestions for improvement.	

F. Aligning classroom observations with evaluation criteria and professional development

See modules 5 and 6 in the handbook.

Professional development should parallel the school improvement plan and evidence of research-based practices in the classroom as determined by systematic classroom observations by the principal and by peers.

In an effective professional development system:

Date:_____ Team: _____

Status (check 1)			
Yes	No	**Success Indicators**	**Action Required**
		The principal compiles reports from classroom observations, showing aggregate areas of strength and areas that need improvement without revealing the identity of individual teachers.	
		The Leadership Team reviews the principal's summary reports of classroom observations and takes them into account in planning professional development.	
		Professional development for teachers includes observations by the principal related to indicators of effective teaching and classroom management.	
		Professional development for teachers includes observations by peers related to indicators of effective teaching and classroom management.	
		Professional development for teachers includes self-assessment related to indicators of effective teaching and classroom management.	
		Teachers are required to make individual professional development plans based on classroom observations.	
		Professional development of individual teachers includes an emphasis on indicators of effective teaching.	
		Professional development for the whole faculty includes assessment of strengths and areas in need of improvement from classroom observations of indicators of effective teaching.	
		Teacher evaluation examines the same indicators used in professional development.	
		The principal plans opportunities for teachers to share their strengths with other teachers.	

G. Helping parents to help their children meet standards

See modules 5 and 6 in the handbook.

The "curriculum of the home" can be much more predictive of academic learning than the family's socioeconomic status. A productive and stimulating home environment includes (1) informed parent-child conversations about school and everyday events; (2) encouragement and discussion of leisure reading; (3) monitoring, discussion, and guidance of television viewing and peer activities; (4) deferral of immediate gratification to accomplish long term goals; (5) expressions of affection and interest in the child's academic and other progress as a person; and perhaps, among such efforts, (6) laughter and spontaneity.

In an effective school:

Date:_____ Team: _____

Status (check 1)			
Yes	No	Success Indicators	Action Required
		Parent policies, activities, and programs cultivate the "curriculum of the home."	
		Parents receive regular communication (absent jargon) about learning standards, their children's progress, and the parents' role in their children's school success.	
		Parents receive practical guidance to maintain regular and supportive verbal interaction with their children.	
		Parents receive practical guidance to maintain daily conversations with their children about their school experiences and progress.	
		Parents receive practical guidance to establish a quiet place for children's studying at home and consistent discipline for studying at home.	
		Parents receive practical guidance to encourage their children's regular reading habits at home.	
		Parents receive practical guidance to model and encourage respectful and responsible behaviors.	
		Parents are given opportunities to meet with each other to share their child-rearing concerns and successes.	
		Parents are given opportunities to meet with teachers to discuss both their children's progress in school and their children's home-based study and reading habits.	

Checklist continues

G. Helping parents to help their children meet standards (continued)

Status (check 1)		Success Indicators	Action Required
Yes	No		
		Parent involvement policies, classroom visit policies, and homework policies are clear, constructive, and frequently communicated to parents and teachers.	
		The faculty, students, and parents regularly discuss the school's Compact that outlines key expectations of students, parents, and teachers.	
		The student report card shows the student's progress in meeting learning standards.	
		The student report card provides parents an opportunity to report on the student's home-based studying and reading habits.	

Stage II: Curriculum, Assessment, and Instructional Planning

A. Engaging teachers in aligning instruction with standards and benchmarks

See modules 5 and 6 in the handbook.

In an effective system, teachers, working in teams, build the taught curriculum from learning standards, curriculum guides, and a variety of resources, including textbooks, other commercial materials, and teacher-created activities and materials. Instructional Teams organize the curriculum into unit plans that guide instruction for all students and for each student. The unit plans assure that students master standards-based objectives and also provide opportunities for enhanced learning.

In a system of teacher team-developed units of instruction:

Date:_____ Team: _____

Status (check 1)		Success Indicators	Action Required
Yes	No		
		Instructional Teams develop standards-aligned units of instruction for each subject and grade level.	
		Units of instruction include standards-based objectives and criteria for mastery.	
		Objectives are leveled to target learning to each student's demonstrated prior mastery based on multiple points of data (i.e., units tests and student work).	

B. Engaging teachers in assessing and monitoring student mastery

See modules 5 and 6 in the handbook. Unit tests are constructed by teachers to give them a good idea of a student's current level of mastery of the objectives without taking a great amount of time to administer. A unit test need not be a pencil and paper test, especially in the lower grades, but is a way for the teacher to specifically check each student's mastery of each objective in a manner that is not time consuming.

Unit pre-tests and post-tests are effective in providing feedback about the instructional system's efficacy when:

Date:_____ Team: _____

Status (check 1)			
Yes	No	Success Indicators	Action Required
		Units of instruction include pre-/post-tests to assess student mastery of standards-based objectives.	
		Unit pre-tests and post-tests are administered to all students in the grade level and subject covered by the unit of instruction.	
		Unit pre-test and post-test results are reviewed by the Instructional Team.	
		Teachers individualize instruction based on pre-test results to provide support for some students and enhanced learning opportunities for others.	
		Teachers re-teach based on post-test results.	

C. Engaging teachers in differentiating and aligning learning activities

See modules 5 and 6 in the handbook.

Learning activities, the assignments given to each student targeted to that student's level of mastery, should be carefully aligned with the objectives included in the unit plan to provide a variety of ways for a student to achieve mastery as evidenced in *both* the successful completion of the learning activities and correct responses on the unit post-test.

In a sound system of individualized learning activities:

Date:_____ Team: _____

Status (check 1)		Success Indicators	Action Required
Yes	No		
		Units of instruction include specific learning activities aligned to objectives.	
		Instructional Teams develop materials for their standards-aligned learning activities and share the materials among themselves.	
		Materials for standards-aligned learning activities are well-organized, labeled, and stored for convenient use by teachers.	

D. Assessing student learning frequently with standards-based assessments

See modules 5 and 6 in the handbook.

Assessment is the process of testing (written, verbal, or by examination of work) to see: (1) what a student knows and can do, and (2) patterns of strengths and weaknesses in what a group of students knows and can do.

In an effective assessment system:

Date:_____ Team: _____

Status (check 1)		Success Indicators	Action Required
Yes	No		
		The school tests every student annually with the same standardized test in basic subject areas so that each student's year-to-year progress can be tracked.	
		The school tests each student at least 3 times each year to determine progress toward standards-based objectives.	
		Teachers receive timely reports of results from standardized and objectives-based tests.	
		The school maintains a central database that includes each student's test scores, placement information, demographic information, attendance, behavior indicators, and other variables useful to teachers.	
		Teams and teachers receive timely reports from the central database to assist in making decisions about each student's placement and instruction.	
		Yearly learning goals are set for the school by the Leadership Team, utilizing student learning data.	
		The Leadership Team monitors school-level student learning data.	
		Instructional Teams use student learning data to assess strengths and weaknesses of the curriculum and instructional strategies.	
		Instructional Teams use student learning data to plan instruction.	
		Instructional Teams use student learning data to identify students in need of instructional support or enhancement.	
		Instructional Teams review the results of unit pre-/post-tests to make decisions about the curriculum and instructional plans and to "red flag" students in need of intervention (both students in need of tutoring or extra help and students needing enhanced learning opportunities because of their early mastery of objectives).	

Stage III: Classroom Instruction

A. Expecting and monitoring sound instruction in a variety of modes

See modules 5 and 6 in the handbook.

A classroom observation and teacher interview instrument to assist teachers in their development of effective teaching methods would include the following items plus those in sections B and C below. Teachers may be observed by other teachers and the principal for purposes of monitoring progress and planning targeted professional development. The items may also be used for teacher self-assessment. By compiling the results for all teachers, a pattern of instructional practices is produced that shows which modes of instruction are most frequently employed and which instructional practices may need focused attention across the faculty.

Date:_____ Team: _____

Status (check 1)		Success Indicators	Action Required
Yes	No		
Preparation			
		The teacher is guided by a document that aligns standards, curriculum, instruction, and assessment.	
		The teacher develops weekly lesson plans based on aligned units of instruction.	
		The teacher uses objectives-based pre-tests.	
		The teacher uses objectives-based post-tests.	
		The teacher maintains a record of each student's mastery of specific learning objectives.	
		The teacher tests frequently using a variety of evaluation methods and maintains a record of the results.	
		The teacher differentiates assignments (individualizes instruction) in response to individual student performance on pre-tests and other methods of assessment.	
Teacher-Directed Whole-Class or Small-Group Instruction			
		Introduction	
		The teacher reviews the previous lesson.	

Checklist continues

A. Expecting and monitoring sound instruction in a variety of modes (continued)

Status (check 1)		Success Indicators	Action Required
Yes	No		
		The teacher clearly states the lesson's topic, theme, and objectives.	
		The teacher stimulates interest in the topics.	
		The teacher uses modeling, demonstration, and graphics.	
		Presentation	
		The teacher proceeds in small steps at a rapid pace.	
		The teacher explains directly and thoroughly.	
		The teacher maintains eye contact.	
		The teacher speaks with expression and uses a variety of vocal tones.	
		The teacher uses prompting/cueing.	
		Summary and Confirmation of Learning	
		The teacher re-teaches when necessary.	
		The teacher reviews with drilling/class recitation.	
		The teacher reviews with questioning.	
		The teacher summarizes key concepts.	
Teacher–Student Interaction			
		The teacher re-teaches following questioning.	
		The teacher uses open-ended questioning and encourages elaboration.	
		The teacher re-directs student questions.	
		The teacher encourages peer interaction.	
		The teacher encourages students to paraphrase, summarize, and relate.	
		The teacher encourages students to check their own comprehension.	
		The teacher verbally praises students.	

A. Expecting and monitoring sound instruction in a variety of modes (continued)

Status (check 1)		Success Indicators	Action Required
Yes	No		
Student-Directed Small-Group and Independent Work			
		The teacher travels to all areas in which students are working.	
		The teacher meets with students to facilitate mastery of objectives.	
		The teacher encourages students to help each other with their work.	
		The teacher interacts instructionally with students (explaining, checking, giving feedback).	
		The teacher interacts managerially with students (reinforcing rules, procedures).	
		The teacher interacts socially with students (noticing and attending to an ill student, asking about the weekend, inquiring about the family).	
		The teacher verbally praises students.	
Computer-Based Instruction			
		Students are engaged and on task.	
		Students are comfortable with the program and its navigation.	
		The teacher travels about the room to assist students.	
		The teacher has documentation of the computer program's alignment with standards-based objectives.	
		The teacher maintains a record of student mastery of standards-based objectives.	
		The teacher assesses student mastery in ways other than those provided by the computer program.	

B. Expecting and monitoring sound homework practices and communication with parents

See modules 5 and 6 in the handbook.

Homework is a primary point of interface between the school and the home, and parents are best able to support the school's purposes for homework when they understand what is expected of students and their role in monitoring their children's homework. Consistency from teacher to teacher and across grade levels and subjects contributes to teachers,' parents,' and students' understanding of the school's purposes for homework and also reinforces students' formation of independent study habits.

In sound homework and parent communication practices:

Date:_____ Team: _____

Status (check 1)		Success Indicators	Action Required
Yes	No		
		The teacher maintains a file of communication with parents.	
		The teacher regularly assigns homework (4 or more days a week).	
		The teacher checks, marks, and returns homework.	
		The teacher includes comments on checked homework.	
		The teacher counts homework toward the student's report card grade.	
		The teacher systematically reports to parents the student's mastery of specific standards-based objectives.	

C. Expecting and monitoring sound classroom management

See modules 5 and 6 in the handbook.

Classroom management is evidenced in the teacher's "withitness," the learner's accountability for learning, the clear procedures in the classroom, and the way the teacher mixes whole-class instruction, small-group instruction, and individual instruction.

Indicators of sound classroom management include:

Date:_____ Team: _____

Status (check 1)		Success Indicators	Action Required
Yes	No		
		When waiting for assistance from the teacher, students are occupied with curriculum-related activities provided by the teacher.	
		Transitions between instructional modes are brief and orderly.	
		Students maintain eye contact and are attentive.	
		Students raise hands or otherwise signal before speaking.	
		The teacher uses a variety of instructional modes.	
		The teacher maintains well-organized student learning materials in the classroom.	
		The teacher displays completed student work in the classroom.	
		The teacher displays classroom rules and procedures in the classroom.	
		The teacher corrects students who do not follow classroom rules and procedures.	
		The teacher reinforces classroom rules and procedures by positively teaching them.	
		The teacher conducts an occasional "behavior check."	
		The teacher engages all students (e.g., encourages silent students to participate).	

Note: All indicator checklists are available for download at www.centerii.org in the section on Restructuring.

Printed in the United States
125589LV00001B/169-266/A

9 781593 117634